Who Shall Not Pass?

Gatekeeping, Communication Theory, and Canadian Media

Who Shall Not Pass?

Gatekeeping, Communication Theory, and Canadian Media

Written by

Kyra Droog
&
Ryan McMillen

with

Austin and Catherine Mardon

GM
★
PRESS

First Printing: 2021

Front/inside cover font: High Tower Text
The Fell Types are digitally reproduced by Igino Marini.

www.iginomarini.com

Cover Design and typeset by Clare Dalton

ISBN 978-1-77369-648-5

E-book ISBN 978-1-77369-649-2

Golden Meteorite Press

103 11919 82 St NW

Edmonton, AB T5B 2W3

www.goldenmeteoritepress.com

Contents

Introduction:
Rhetoric
and
Communication

Communication is a wonderful and terrible thing. It can bring people together and tear them apart; denote happiness and love, hate and war. The ability for us to communicate with each other is absolutely incredible because it allows us to make the intangible, tangible. It is, unquestionably, the greatest tool that we as humans have been provided. There has been an argument for decades over whether the pen is stronger than the sword or vice versa, when in fact, it is the word that is stronger than both. Words start and end wars, they create connection and disconnect, and most importantly, they help us understand each other as humans - ideally so that we can share our lived experiences with each other to help propel our world forward.

As we begin our journey into this book, it is important for us to do so with the clearest of understandings regarding communication itself. For that reason, we will be taking some time to explore the concept of communication: what it constitutes, how it functions, and what can get in its way that can lead to miscommunication and confusion. This discussion will lead us into an even deeper method of understanding communication, particularly in terms of gatekeeping and media: rhetoric. We will take some time to explore the concept of rhetoric to ensure we understand the differences between rhetoric and communication, and how we can begin to notice when rhetoric is being used within communication. From there, we will learn about Canadian communication theory, so as we dive into specific theories and theorists, we have the context to understand what they were thinking and why. Finally, we will take a brief moment to note some important aspects of this book before we jump into our first chapter.

Now, before we begin exploring the concept of communication in great detail, we authors have an important note to provide you readers with. This book is in no way intended to be a comprehensive analysis of gatekeeping in all forms of digital and print media: to do so would require a library full of books and lifetimes of analyses. Our intention with this book is to provide a glimpse into the complex and confusing world of gatekeeping using the lens of Canadian digital and print media. This glimpse might be enough for some people, but others may feel empowered to continue their learning and further explore what is and isn't available in Canada in terms of digital and print media, and continue to wonder why. We want to remind you that no one book, blog, or film is going to have all the answers, and that this is just a look into a complicated past, present, and future of gatekeeping in Canadian media. With this disclaimer in mind, let us take some time to remind ourselves about the concept of communication and how we will consider it within this book.

A Brief Introduction to Communication

Everyone in this world thinks that they know what communication is. That doesn't, however, mean that everyone actually understands communication in the global context in which it exists, nor does it mean that everyone can break the concept of communication down to its very building blocks and explain why it is one of the most important functions of human existence. For this reason, we're going to begin this book by making sure that when we refer to communication throughout this book, you as a reader understand exactly what we're talking about. By doing so, we are ensuring that our dialogue remains open and that our explanations are able to be understood on the deepest of levels. After all, it doesn't make much sense to have a conversation about a topic before first ensuring that everyone is on the same page about their understanding of the topic itself.

Of course, there are hundreds upon hundreds of definitions of communication, all of which are technically correct depending on the way in which communication is being viewed in that circumstance. Communication is a truly multi-faceted concept, which inevitably leads to multiple, correct definitions of the same term. That said, there is one definition of communication that is preferred by these authors, and will be utilized for the remainder of this book. In their book *A First Look at Communication Theory*, Em Griffin and his colleagues defined communication as "the relational process of creating and interpreting messages that elicit a response" (2015, p. 6). This definition is particularly overarching, because it references the three most important aspects of communication: the creation of a message, the interpretation of the message, and the response elicited from the message. As we will learn, there are many pieces that come together to create what we know as communication; in fact, let's take some time to explore some of those pieces now.

Em Griffin and his colleagues suggest that there are five main features of communication that are notable when studying communication. It is these five features that we will begin with in our journey to understand the concept of communication. We'll start with exploring one of the most basic yet most important aspects of communication: the message. Understanding what constitutes a message and a message's basic purpose are essential to our ability to not only understand the building blocks of communication, but also the ways in which messages impact communication as regards gatekeeping in Canadian media. So what constitutes a message, exactly? Much like communication, there are a wide variety of definitions for messages. For the purposes of this book, a message will be "a text including signs, symbols, and/or information intended for analysis by a recipient." According to this definition, which was put together by the authors of this book, a message could be a wide variety of things. It would be helpful, then, to break the concept of a message down further, and look at the idea of a text.

According to Em Griffin and his colleagues, a text is "a record of a message that can be analyzed by others; for example, a book, film, photograph, or any transcript or recording of a speech or broadcast" (2015, p. 7). A message, then, takes the form of a text, which is then analyzed. Consider a song: a song is a message, because it is built of signs, symbols, and information and is intended to be analyzed by audiences. Beatles songs, for example, have been under intense scrutiny to find hidden meanings behind the words, even though the Beatles were insistent that no hidden meanings existed. We can also consider a book; for example, Phillip Pullman's *The Golden Compass* is not only a story - it is also a religious allegory that speaks to Pullman's thoughts on religion. Of course, these are more complicated examples of communication; after all, everything from a short text message to a note left on the fridge to a photograph constitutes a text under Griffin's definition.

Texts with messages make up the most basic building blocks of communication. Shortly, we will consider the communication cycle, but before we do so, we will continue our exploration of Griffin's five main features of communication. Messages make up the first feature of communication, and the second feature is the creation of messages. To understand this concept, let's consider a situation in which we would need to craft a message. If, for example, we needed to let a friend know that their actions were hurtful to us, we would have a few ways to share that message. We could send them a text; sharing only our words and leaving our tone, body language, and more to the receiver to interpret. We could give them a call, in which case they could hear our words and our tone, but be unsure of our body language. We could arrange to meet them in person to discuss, where words, tone, and body language would be available for interpretation. As we consider the best way to craft a message to our friend, we would be thinking about what the most important message is to get across to this friend. Maybe we're done with the friendship in general, and a text is the easiest way to share the information. Maybe we want to mend the relationship, and we want to meet in person so that our friend can see exactly how much they hurt us. There are a huge amount of considerations that we make when we craft a message, and these considerations have repercussions when it comes to the interpretation of the messages.

Message interpretation is the third feature in Griffin's list. If we consider the same situation we did for message creation in regards to interpretation, we can see exactly how difficult it can be to interpret a message's intention without having all the facts. Interpreting a text message or written note can be particularly difficult because all we have are the words on the page; we don't know if the intention was cynical, sarcastic, or wholesome. In the same way, though we can hear a person's tone in a phone call, we're never sure if that's the whole story. In-person communication provides the most effective creation and interpretation of messages, because both parties are able to consider tone, body language, and words and interpret the message based on those factors. Of course, in-person communication isn't always an option, but it is one of the most effective communication situations.

Communication is a relational process, as Griffin reminds us in his fourth feature. Messages aren't created in a vacuum - they are created with the intention of sharing them with other people. When the Beatles wrote a song, for example, they wrote it for a purpose. *Glass Onion*, for example, was written with the intention of mocking the people who read into Beatles songs looking for deeper meaning regarding things like the "Paul is Dead" conspiracy theory. When you send a text to your friend, you aren't sending the text for your benefit: your intention is that your friend reads the text message and responds to you. Authors write books with their ideal readers in mind. Television shows and movies are written, directed, and produced with their viewers and fans in their minds. Communication is a collective process, involving a minimum of two people, something that needs to be kept in mind as we move forward in our understanding of communication.

Griffin's final feature of communication reminds us that messages are intended to elicit a response. Songs are intended to make us feel a certain way. Movies tug at our heartstrings or make us laugh, depending on their intention. An image can make us feel homesick or heartbroken. A text message can bring us great joy or great sadness. Whether the response is a communication in return or an emotion or a general reaction, when it comes down to it, the purpose of a message is to encourage a response. When you text your friend a photo, you want them to laugh. Whether they text you and tell you they thought it was funny or not is essentially irrelevant; your message accomplished its purpose when your friend let out a snorting laugh as they saw the picture.

Now that we've taken a short while to explore some of the most important features of communication, let's take some time to look over one of the most popular and recognized communication theories: the Shannon & Weaver model of communication. Exploring this model of communication will help us put our understanding of communication into an even better position, helping us to critically analyze gatekeeping in Canadian media. In addition, this model of communication will help us better understand the communication that we undertake each and every day.

The Shannon & Weaver model of communication focuses around five aspects of communication: sender, receiver, channel, encoder, and decoder. The channel, of course, functions as the medium through which the message is sent. The sender, or the person sending the message, encodes the message in a way that is appropriate for the channel. When they send the message, the receiver, or the person for whom the message was intended, decodes and comprehends the message. To better understand the Shannon & Weaver model of communication, see the image below:

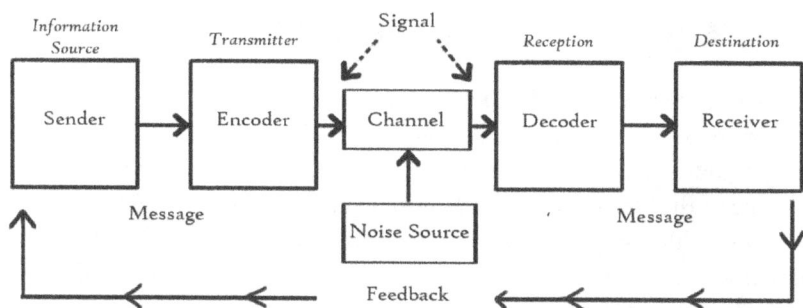

Image 1: The Shannon & Weaver Model of Communication

Now, as we all know, communication isn't that simple: there are lots of things that can go wrong and result in misunderstandings. Shannon & Weaver highlight noise, or a type of disturbance that results in the message not being received as it was sent. Let's look at a few examples of how noise could work. Actual, physical noise can impede communication: for example, if the authors were yelling at the reader from across the street, it would be difficult for the reader to hear the authors. If a bus drove by while the authors were yelling this section of the book to the reader, the reader might not understand any of it due to the noise of the bus, and make it the rest of the way through this book without any understanding of the Shannon & Weaver model of communication whatsoever. If the reader was speaking to their friend on the phone but the service cut out for a minute, the reader might not understand exactly what their friend was saying because they missed a few key words.

As we are about to learn, there are a multitude of ways in which to understand communication through a variety of communication theories, which we will soon explore. That said, it is time for us to dive into a form of communication that will certainly find itself under the proverbial microscope during our exploration of gatekeeping in Canadian media. Rhetoric, as we will learn, is essential to the human experience, and is therefore an important piece of the puzzle when it comes to communicating (or not communicating) gatekeeping decisions to the general public. Without further ado, let's turn our attention to rhetoric, one of the most fascinating facets of communication to study.

A Brief Introduction to Rhetoric

There is no better way to introduce rhetoric than the way in which Edward Corbett & Robert Connors introduce rhetoric in their book *Classical Rhetoric for the Modern Student: Fourth Edition*. According to Corbett and Connors: "rhetoric is the art or the discipline that deals with the use of discourse, either spoken or written, to inform or persuade or motivate an audience, whether that audience is made up of one person or a group of persons" (1999, p. I). As with any definition, the aforementioned definition will require some unpacking to ensure we fully understand the scope of rhetoric.

To begin our analysis of this definition, let us pick up on the way in which rhetoric is described: as an art or the discipline. Now, many people might take a moment to consider the dichotomy between those two terms, because for the most part, the concepts of art and discipline are reasonably separate. There is a fair amount of discourse surrounding the connection of the freeing power of art to the structure of a discipline, which can be summed up through the general understanding that even something as free and objective as art typically demonstrates some form of structure or connection. To understand this concept better, let's take an example stemming from the visual arts: "concepts like lighting, the horizon line, and perspective are essential parts of the foundation needed for the creation of a proper composition in an area like visual arts; artists follow these basic rule to connect their art and simultaneously explore the options and possibility surrounding these rules" (Vargas, 2019). Whether the rules are built to follow or to break, there are basic understandings and rules within visual arts that exist to aid in the way a piece of art is interpreted.

In a similar way, rhetoric is both an art and a discipline: it is beautiful and melodic like music, but strategically either follows or breaks a set of basic norms. We will take a moment to explore some of the most basic structures of rhetoric shortly, but for this moment, knowing that rhetoric - though it functions in a variety of ways - typically exists within set structures is exactly what we need. Rhetoric is, therefore, both an art and a discipline; as we continue to explore rhetoric further, we will better be able to understand exactly why this is the case.

We should take a moment to appreciate that Corbett and Connors' definition of rhetoric denotes that rhetoric is traditionally found in written or spoken discourse; as we will learn, rhetoric found its roots in Ancient Greece, where the pen and voice were powerful rhetorical weapons. If we think about it, written and spoken words cover most if not all of the ways in which we communicate even today: written notes, texting, and even memes count as the written word, and video calls, phone calls, and other forms of virtual connection fall within the spoken word category. By specifying the parameters of rhetoric, Corbett and Connors are ensuring that as readers, we understand exactly what does and does not constitute rhetoric within specific media.

Inform, persuade, or motivate: these are the three reasons that Corbett and Connors suggest rhetoric would be used. These three categories take up a substantial amount of the communication that we take on each and every day. We inform our clients of progress on their projects, we persuade our bosses to give us pay raises or days off, and we motivate ourselves to get our work done quickly so we have extra time at the end of the day to relax. We inform our partners what we would like to eat for dinner, we persuade them to sit down and enjoy a moment with us, and we motivate them to be their best selves. We inform ourselves through reading the news or an interesting book, we persuade ourselves to skip the bowl of chips in favour of a salad, and we motivate ourselves to go for a run or a bike ride because we know that we will enjoy the endorphins that are associated with physical activity. Outside of small-talk, giving basic directions, exclamations like "oh my gosh!" and other short and reasonably forgettable forms of communication, rhetoric is a functional and fundamental part of our everyday lives.

The final portion of Corbett and Connors' definition stipulates that the audience that we are communicating to can be made up of a single individual or a large group. Think about the last rousing speech you heard: that was rhetoric. Consider the last time a close friend or family member convinced you that you should go to an event that you really didn't want to attend. Both of these examples count as rhetoric, helping demonstrate just how entrenched rhetoric is within our society. It is interesting, then, that many people don't know exactly what rhetoric is or how powerful it is. For our own knowledge, and for assistance in understanding some discussions later on in this book, let's now take some time to explore the five parts, or canons, of rhetoric.

In *De Inventione*, the Roman philosopher Cicero explains that there are five canons, or tenets, of rhetoric: invention, arrangement, style, memory, and delivery. Although these canons were originally created with a focus on oratory, or public speaking, most are also applicable to the writing process stages of prewriting, drafting, and rewriting (University of Arkansas, n.d.).

The five canons of rhetoric are extremely important to our understanding of rhetoric, and the upcoming three types of persuasive discourse, so let's take a moment to understand each of the canons of rhetoric. The first canon, invention, or *inventio*, is exactly what it sounds like: inventing the material to deliver. This is the brainstorming stage that most authors both revel in and absolutely despise: the time wherein there are no limits to creativity, but when we are forced to consider what is realistic and achievable and what is simply out of scope at this point in time. This stage could include coming up with a compelling idea for a paper, doing some research to see if you know enough about rhetoric to write a whole book on it, or using a whiteboard to create a brain map for a new non-fiction book.

The second canon, arrangement (also known as disposition or *dispositio*), is also fairly self-explanatory: taking the ideas that we came up with in the first stage and arranging them in the most compelling way possible. This is the oft-dreaded outlining stage, where we take ideas and formulate them in a comprehensible manner. Whether you're outlining a book, an essay, or an argument as to why you should or shouldn't get your nose pierced, if you are taking your points of discussion and arranging them in the order you feel is most effective and compelling, you're engaged in the arrangement/ disposition stage of rhetoric.

Elocution, or *elocutio*, is the third canon of rhetoric. Interestingly, if you'd mentioned the elocution canon to a rhetorician from Ancient Greece, they would understand something very different than what we intend. Corbett & Connors explain:

We associate the word [elocution] with the act of speaking (hence, the elocution contest). This notion of speaking, of course, implicit in the Latin verb from which this word stems, *loqui*, "to speak" [...]. It was after the revival of interest in delivery in the second half of the eighteenth century that the word elocution began to take on its present meaning. But for the classical rhetorician, *elocutio* meant "style" (Corbett & Connors, 1999, p. 21).

There is, of course, a distinct connection between elocution and style, though the concept of style is notoriously difficult to define in a rhetorical sense. The authors of this book believe that the best way to understand style is to provide two examples of very distinct styles, and to analyze the differences in speech. Doing so will help us understand in no uncertain terms what the concept of style is as it applies to rhetoric. For example, choose any two American presidents - if you listen to their inaugural speeches, you will see their unique styles. Where they pause between words, how they linger on or gloss over specific words or phrases, and importantly, where they place the impact on specific words or phrases. If you watch and listen carefully, you will be able to discern their individual styles, and even begin to anticipate them as their speeches continue. In general, however, elocution involves an analysis of the way in which rhetoric is presented. As you read through this book, look for the specific styles that the authors utilize while they write: it may even assist you in knowing which sections of the book were written by which author. Specific word choice, placement of commas, and even the practice of starting sentences with lists are specific stylistic choices that can be analyzed for effectiveness under the canon of elocution.

The fourth canon of rhetoric is that of memory, or *memoria*. This canon focuses on the memorizing of verbal presentations, whether they are speeches, parts in a play, or lines from poetry. Though the technical need for memorizing speeches is slowly diminishing thanks to technology like teleprompters that can provide the facade of memorization, in Ancient Greece, the art of memorizing speeches was taken particularly seriously. Of course, it is difficult to know exactly how much of a speech a person has memorized before giving the speech unless either it is clear they have no idea what they are supposed to say next, or you have a copy of their speech in front of you and are comparing the words on the page to the words coming out of their mouth. Memory is an aspect of rhetoric that we will not be too focused on in our study, but that's not to say that it isn't important, both to us and to the Ancient Greek rhetoricians.

The final canon of rhetoric is delivery, or *pronuntiatio*. Delivery, or the process of sharing a piece of (often verbal) rhetoric with an individual or group, is similar to memory in the way it was often not considered in the writing about rhetoric in Ancient Greece; however, at the time, nothing was more important than delivery. We've all heard great speeches and we've all heard terrible speeches. Speech material aside, the differentiation between a great and terrible speech predominantly comes from delivery. Is the speech given confidently? Is the speaker stammering and consistently checking their notes? Does the speaker instil a sense of peace in their listeners, or do they feel agitated? Being able to impact the audience emotionally, and make them feel a particular way is one way of demonstrating the power of delivery, and the prowess of a speaker.

Corbett & Connors make an important note about the importance of delivery before the invention of the printing press:

Involved in the treatment of delivery was concern for the management of the voice and for gestures (*actio*). Precepts were laid down about the modulation of the voice for the proper pitch, volume, and emphasis and about pausing and phrasing. In regard to action, orators were trained in gesturing, in the proper stance and posture of the body, and in the management of the eyes and facial expressions (Corbett & Connors, 1999, p. 22).

Let's discuss the real importance of delivery using a practical example. Consider, for example, that you are trying to convince your friends that they should skip work and come with you to Disneyland for a week-long holiday. Are you going to be more convincing if your speech is punctuated with "I guess" and "well I think it would be fun" and "but only if you want to," or if you use more assertive terms like "it will be an absolute blast" and "you have the vacation time anyway" and "I'll help you fake mono"? Of course, the authors of this book can only condone utilizing rhetoric for the most nobel of intentions, but this example proves the importance of delivery: one method of delivery is guaranteed to be more effective than the other - though whether or not it is effective enough to convince your friends to come to Disneyland with you depends on a variety of other factors as well.

Now that we've had the opportunity to explore the five canons of rhetoric, it's time to look into the three main kinds of rhetorical discourse. These are the most common ways in which rhetoric is utilized, and each type assists in the effectiveness of the persuasion intended. As we continue through this book, it will be helpful to be able to establish which of the three main kinds of rhetorical discourse are applicable to our discussions about gatekeeping and media. By recognizing these types of discourse, we can better understand what makes or made particular gatekeeping discussions or decisions effective or ineffective.

The first kind of rhetorical discourse we will explore is deliberative rhetoric, or "discourse in which we seek to persuade someone to do something or accept our point of view" (Corbett & Connors, 1999, p. 23). This form of rhetoric is always concerned about the future: whether or not we will do something, whether or not we will believe something, or whether or not we will function in a certain way are all future-focused examples of deliberative rhetoric. Let's consider, for example, that we were having a discussion with one of our friends, who doesn't like having to slow down on the highway as they pass a tow truck or a police car that's stopped on the shoulder with their lights on. You would use a deliberative rhetorical lens while providing them with evidence and reasons that regardless of whether or not they like slowing down, that they should be slowing down; not only because it's the law, but also because it's the right thing to do. In the end, your goal is to persuade them to do something (slow down when a police officer or tow truck is pulled over on the side of the road with their lights on) and to accept your point of view (that slowing down in that case is the right thing to do). Advertising, political speeches, and most presentations and proposals fall under deliberative rhetorical discourse.

The second kind of rhetorical discourse that we will discuss is forensic or judicial rhetoric. This form of rhetoric is focused on either accusing or defending; typically in reference to a court of law. Whereas deliberative discourse exists in the future, forensic rhetoric exists in the past: we are looking to prove that, in the past, our client didn't commit a crime, or that the person we are prosecuting did, in fact, commit that crime. Think about any courtroom drama you have ever watched. In the courtroom, the defense attorney was using a forensic rhetorical argument to prove that their client is innocent of the crime, and the prosecution lawyer is using a forensic rhetorical argument to prove that the accused did commit the crime. These arguments are typically as evidence-based as possible, though they do involve a fair amount of storytelling, particularly when the rhetoric is being witnessed by a jury. Forensic rhetoric isn't only used in the courtroom, though: it also exists in the writing and amending of laws and other such policy, and even in personal justifications, like defending your decision to ignore your friend's phone call to finish watching the movie you are halfway through.

The third and final type of rhetorical discourse we are exploring here is that of epideictic rhetoric. Epideictic rhetoric has a focus on the present; in the exact moment during which we are presenting our rhetoric to a person or group. This form of rhetoric is typically used in ceremonial occasions, such as commencement speeches, eulogies, and awards presentations. If you were giving a speech to a group of recent graduates, encouraging and exciting them about their future, that would be a form of epideictic rhetoric. If you were standing in front of a crowd telling them about how wonderful your late family member was, that would also be a form of epideictic rhetoric. This form of rhetoric is no less common than the aforementioned two, but it does have an important amount of connection and emotion present in the argument.

Of course, we could delve much more deeply into these forms of rhetoric, but for the purposes of this book, understanding the basic outline of the forms is plenty. We have one further rhetorical focus to explore before moving on from the topic, and that is the five parts of the classical argument: the time-proven structure of most rhetorical arguments that presents the most effective argument.

The introduction to a rhetorical argument, also known as the exordium, presents the most difficult and important part of rhetorical discussion. In the introduction, the rhetorician's focus is on creating ethos, or moral character; essentially, proving that they are worthy of trust, and that the reader or listener should listen to them. This section is where the rhetorician provides information about themselves and their topic to the audience, establishing their credibility and authority (or lack thereof) to discuss the topic, while also counteracting any pre-existing prejudices or misunderstandings about the rhetorician or the subject of discussion (Lees, 2016). Of course, it would seem that the easiest way to do so would be to provide a list of credentials and reasons why a rhetorician is qualified to discuss a specific topic, but that's not how the introduction typically functions. By the end of an introduction, audiences want to feel like they know the rhetorician, and that they have a good reason to inherently trust and listen to this individual. Cultivating this relationship with an audience, particularly in such a small time, is difficult, and it is a true test of a rhetorician's grit to see if they can create that understanding and trust.

In addition to creating ethos, the introduction or exordium provides a few more important pieces of information for the audience. This section of the rhetorical argument introduces the subject matter, prepares the audience to critically think about the subject matter, and shares the rhetorician's position on the topic at hand. Now, readers, we can hear you wondering how a rhetorician is supposed to fit all that information into a single paragraph. The wonderful thing about rhetorical discussions is that though there is somewhat of a structure, the length of that structure is reasonably fluid - a rhetorician can take as much or as little time as they would need to integrate themselves, their topic, and their position with their audience. Doing so successfully is paramount to the rest of their argument, so it is in this section that much of their time is spent.

The second part of the five-part classical argument is the narration, or narratio. This section provides the facts, and nothing but the facts, to the audience so that they are further posed to think critically about the topic at hand. The key to the narration section is that the information is expository, not argumentative. Even though the purpose of a rhetorical argument is exactly that - argument - the purpose of the narration section is to provide the audience with the unquestioned facts, without spinning them in a way that suits a rhetorician's argument. This section sets the issue in context, provides context and limits around the scope of the argument, and importantly, states the thesis for the topic (Lees, 2016). That said, this section should be brief: the rhetorician will be diving into the topic in later sections, so all that needs to be provided here are the facts necessary for the audience to understand what is at stake for this discussion. Is this an argument against capital punishment for someone accused of murder? Is this an argument for or against a women's right to an abortion? Is this argument for or against the opportunity for a teen to go to a late-night party? Each rhetorical argument will have different stakes, and it's important for the audience to understand those stakes early on in the argument.

Confirmation, or the third part of the five-part classical argument, is where the argument itself exists. Unlike in the narration, the confirmation section is where rhetoricians prove their argument - providing the facts that support their stance, and encouraging their audiences to support that stance alongside them. This section is particularly artistic in its craft, as it's not just a matter of dumping every piece of proof into a paragraph or two; instead, it's about proof stacking on proof, and finding the perfect order upon which to present proof to create the most impact in the audience. The confirmation is never complete until the entire rhetorical argument is complete: rhetoricians must return to the confirmation section as they craft each of the other sections to ensure that the confirmation is as strong and convincing as possible. Outside of ensuring that an audience trusts a rhetorician, there's nothing more important than the confirmation of an argument in rhetorical argumentation.

The only thing better than proving an argument that you support is disproving the opposite argument, further strengthening your argument. The confirmation section does exactly that; refuting the opposition's argument in order to strengthen the original argument. This is the section that allows rhetoricians to provide the opposing argument before disproving it. The key to ensuring this section remains successful is respectfully disproving the opposing argument - not completely trashing it. Though rhetoric is argumentative in nature, it is a respectful form of argumentation. Part of the way in which a rhetorician earns their ethos is through recognizing the opposition's argument and disproving it in a way that recognizes the legitimacy of the opposition, even though they are at the same time proving it wrong.

That said, let's consider the fourth section of the five-part classical argument: the refutation. The refutation is an important part of building ethos for a rhetorician, as it is the section wherein a rhetorician concedes to an opponent's argument. This is not only a powerful ethical appeal for the rhetorician, but it also allows the rhetorician to use powerful sentence structure like "though my opponent is correct in believing that [...], one true assertion does not an argument make" (Lees, 2016). The key to the refutation is ensuring that the opposition's argument is characterized correctly, because incorrectly representing their argument would be detrimental to a rhetorician's ethical appeal. The refutation also needs to be an argument that the audience will be thinking about, and not a silly or insignificant argument: the argument that will be conceded needs to be strong and poignant in order to create a successful ethical appeal as well as a stronger argument against the point that follows the refutation. Now, depending on the strength of the refutation, this section can live before or after the confirmation; in rhetorical argumentation, the placement of these two sections depends entirely on their strength and effectiveness.

The final section is referred to as the conclusion, or the peroration. The peroration is often considered the climax of the rhetorical argument, in that it is the most effective point at which to utilize emotional appeals and ensure that the audience is emotionally connected to a rhetorician's argument. Emphasizing the relevance of the argument at hand and sharing the way in which the audience can take action to support an action are just some ways that the peroration can exist. Of course, rhetoricians want to continue to have their audiences trust them throughout the entire rhetorical argument, so ensuring that audiences remain favourable to their position and have a full understanding of the argument and the stakes are particularly important. Much like the first lines of a rhetorical argument, the final lines can make or break an argument, and though it is expected that rhetoricians put blood, sweat, and tears into crafting the perfect conclusion, that work should never be seen in the actual rhetoric - it should seem as if the conclusion was effortless simply because the argument is irrefutably correct.

Our understanding of the five parts of the classical argument is more important than just for the purposes of this book: now, we will be able to effectively apply this knowledge in our everyday lives. In doing so, we will be able to understand, analyze, and question the ways in which arguments are presented to us, and come to realize why some arguments feel more effective than others. Rhetoric overall is a powerful tool, when used correctly, and it is a tool that is particularly important in the realms of communication theory and gatekeeping.

Now that we've had an opportunity to take a brief dive into rhetoric, let's move on to the final aspect of our introductory section: taking some time to learn about Canadian communication theory, which will help us lay the groundwork for our discussions about digital and print media, gatekeeping, and Canadian media. Doing so will not only give us a deeper understanding of the theorists that we will be discussing, but will also help us understand why it's important that we consider Canadian communication theory, and why studying aspects like gatekeeping makes particular sense through theory; in particular, communication theory.

A Brief Introduction to Canadian Communication Theory

Canadian communication theory is a particularly fascinating discipline, not only because of its roots and history, but also because of the results when Canadian communication theory is applied to Canadian media. It makes good sense, then, to begin by exploring Canadian communication theorists, and some of the key differences between Canadian communication theory, and communication theory across the globe; in particular, the United States of America. Doing so will not only help you, our dear readers, understand why we are specifically considering gatekeeping in Canadian media through a Canadian communication theory lens, but will also provide us with key context for our discussions as we continue through this book.

This brief introduction will give us the opportunity to preview some of the communication theorists and theories that we will be discussing in later chapters of this book. Going into our exploration with a basic understanding of these theories and theorists will aid us in engaging in a well-rounded and critical exploration of gatekeeping vs censorship in Chapter 1, and will then help us consider these theories and theorists on a deeper level once we reach their respective sections. We will also explore some of the ways in which communication theory is different for Canada than it is for the rest of the world, which will help us understand why it makes most sense to consider Canadian communication theory and theorists in our discussion of Canadian media and gatekeeping.

Of course, in order to have context for Canadian communication theory, there are some specific understandings about Canada itself that we need to bring to light. Canada is a particularly unique country when it comes to communication, which is just one reason why Canadian communication theory plays such a vital part in communication theories around the world. When most people think about Canada, they think about nature: big lakes, vast forests, and ice-cold tundras. To a point, those preconceptions are true, because Canada is an expansive country with absolutely beautiful and breathtaking landscapes. Harold Adams Innis, famous Canadian communication theorist, considered Canadian communication theory through the lens of its infrastructure and how the country was built. He argued that the building of the railway was an expansion of communication; after all, cross-country communication flowed much more smoothly and much faster after the railway was complete.

It's likely that everyone reading this book has heard of Marshall McLuhan, whether in a formal, school setting or even just heard his name in passing. Marshall McLuhan is one of the most well-known Canadian communication theorists, and he is the one that coined the expression "the media is the message." We will be taking some time to explore the implications of this expression, as well as the ways in which his theories impact the ways in which media and information are passed to us, and how the media that provides the information can occasionally skew the message itself. This discussion will particularly impact the way in which we discuss various types of print and digital media, and will take us into some fascinating examples and new ways to consider the way in which we receive important messages.

Though the word 'propaganda' has had a negative connotation cast over it, stemming from Nazi Germany and World War II, Canadian communication theorist John Grierson worked with the concept of propaganda in a more positive light. Exploring his theory of democratic propaganda will engage us in some critical thinking about the ethics and intentions of propaganda, and when it is and is not acceptable for governments and other governing bodies to manage the flow of information to the people. We'll also be considering Grierson's work in-depth when we consider documentary film, as Grierson is known as the father of documentary film in Canada. By examining his theories and his work in documentary film, we will be able to garner a better understanding of what his ideas of gatekeeping, censorship, and propaganda resulted in, for Canadian documentaries.

Though Gertrude Joch Robinson was not born in Canada, her work on Canadian communication theory is undeniable. She explored the question of truth - what is true? - and who decides the truth that is shared with the general public. The roots of her theories live within symbolic interactionism, which we will be learning about in a future chapter, but her theories themselves are particularly impactful both to Canadian communication theory, and to our broader discussion around Canadian media, communication theory, and gatekeeping. Her theories will get us thinking about what is true, and how we establish what is true, particularly during a time where the truth can be masked and altered by the medium through which it is presented. How difficult is it to establish the real truth? Thanks to Gertrude Joch Robinson's work, we will have the opportunity to consider the ways in which we see the truth.

As we will learn when we discuss Harold Adams Innis and his theories in detail, Canadian communication theory is unique in part because of the way in which the country exists. Before the advent of technology like cell phones and the internet, and with such space between communities, communicating over long distances was particularly difficult. Because of this, Canadian communication theory exists with the landscapes, space, and terrain of Canada in mind; without the challenges that the Canadian landscape posed on early communicators, Canadian communication theory would look very different today. That isn't the biggest difference between Canadian communication theory and other communication theories, though - it is just one that we need to keep in the back of our minds as we travel towards a greater understanding of why Canadian communication theory exists in the ways it does.

One of the biggest differences between Canadian and American communication theories is the emphasis placed on the view of, or reason for, the communication. As one would expect, American communication theories are predominantly driven by market needs, or the ability to transfer product or other information from one place to another (Shade, n.d.). This concept follows the transportation model, which includes "a tendency toward a centralization of decision-making and authority while decentralizing work; the dominance of global corporations over local organizations; and a consequent homogeneity of participants and content" (Shade, n.d.). This is the focus that lives behind the purpose of communication in America: the ability to transport messages, products, and more with the intent to fulfill market needs.

Canada, on the other hand, has a deeper focus than that of market needs. As Leslie Shade explains: "communications technology and theory has been important to Canada and Canadians because of the importance of its vast geography, its geographical proximity to the U.S., and its cultural and bilingual diversity" (Shade, n.d.). Canada's geography and landscape is essential to the way in which communication occurs within the country, providing a deeper sense of cultural importance within communication. For this reason, culture is fundamentally imbued within communication and communication theory in Canada, where it isn't so in the United States. Robert Babe argues that: "it is expected that mainstream Canadian communication theorists will show greater affinity to the 'culture as communication' model than their U.S. colleagues, who will be more attracted to the relatively more individualistic 'transmission model'" (Babe, 2014, p. 24).

We could talk about the fundamental differences between Canada and the United States, both in terms of culture and communication theory, for an entire book; for now, we need to understand that the underlying cause and focus of communication is one way that sets Canada and the United States apart in terms of communication theory. We will continue to discuss the importance of culture within Canadian communication and

Canadian communication theory as we move into chapter two, when we discuss the thought of Harold Adams Innis, but for now, we have the basic understanding of one of the major distinctions between Canadian and American communication thought.

Now that we've taken the time to briefly introduce ourselves to the concepts and thoughts of Canadian communication theory and theorists, we can move forward to the final section of our introduction: navigating this book. This section will provide a brief overview of what can be expected through the remainder of the book, and will segue us between the brief introductions to topics we have touched on so far, and the far deeper and more in-depth conversations that we are moving towards.

Navigating this Book

The authors of this book believe firmly in the importance of context in learning and understanding new concepts. For that reason, each chapter will begin, much like the introductory section did, with an exploration of definitions and concepts that will aid readers in the understanding of specific aspects of the section we will then be exploring. We'll begin with an exploration of the difference, in definition and in function, between gatekeeping, censorship, and propaganda. Exploring and understanding these three concepts is fundamental to understanding the remainder of the book's explorations, as though the terms gatekeeping, censorship, and propaganda are often used interchangeably, the fact remains that they represent very different concepts. Our second chapter will delve into the world of print media, exploring exactly what constitutes print media before looking at print media and gatekeeping through the lenses of four different Canadian communication theorists.

After print media, we will take the time to explore digital media, in relation to documentary film, film and television, and radio. Our exploration of digital media will utilize strictly Canadian examples, and will also be backed through theories provided by some of the most recognized and popular communication theorists. Then, we will move on to exploring the ethics of gatekeeping, and consider two questions: who, and why. Who has the power to make gatekeeping decisions? Why are gatekeeping decisions made the way they are? Finally, we will wrap up the book by considering gatekeeping in our own world. By wondering how we can impact and consider gatekeeping in our own worlds, we will be able to take our discussion full circle in our exploration of gatekeeping, Canadian media, and Canadian communication theory.

Chapter 1: Gatekeeping, Censorship, and Propaganda

There are many preconceptions - and also misconceptions - when it comes to what constitutes gatekeeping, censorship, and propaganda. Though many people equate the three terms, they are actually very different, and before we go into exploring the concept of gatekeeping within digital and print media, it follows that we have to first understand the differences between gatekeeping, censorship, and propaganda. Now, this understanding isn't as simple as reading the definitions of the three terms; in fact, there is a lot more context to explore before we jump into the next sections. Doing so will ensure we have a well-rounded basis of understanding that will further our comprehension of the following chapters.

We'll begin by exploring technical definitions of gatekeeping, censorship, and propaganda, and looking at the ways in which they are similar and different. Doing so will lead us into a functional exploration of the differences between gatekeeping, censorship, and propaganda: here, we will explore different scenarios to help cement our understanding of their differences and similarities. This understanding, then, will lead us into our explorations of print and digital media.

Like many other terms, gatekeeping, censorship, and propaganda have a wide variety of definitions, all of which have varying degrees of difference. For that reason, we won't just consider one definition of each term; instead, we will consider three, which will give us a well-rounded understanding of the variances in meaning behind each term. As we have mentioned many times before, and will definitely mention again, the key to deeper understanding of new concepts is context, and exploring the contexts of these definitions and concepts will guide our understanding of the remainder of this book.

According to the Cambridge Dictionary, gatekeeping refers to "the activity of trying to control who gets particular resources, power, or opportunities, and who does not" (2021). This definition is fairly straightforward, and does note that gatekeeping covers a wide range of activities, with the main focus on the fact that the gatekeeper is attempting to control access. Interesting is the use of the phrase 'trying to control;' after all, the phrase 'gatekeeping' is most often utilized when the controlling of access is either already in progress or already completed. That said, particularly when it comes to news media, the phrase 'gatekeeping' is often utilized during news investigations when it appears as if a company or government is attempting to keep certain information under wraps, though the journalists feel it is imperative to share that information with the public.

Urban Dictionary refers to gatekeeping in a different manner, suggesting that gatekeeping occurs "when someone takes it upon themselves to decide who does or does not have access or rights to a community or identity" (2012). Whereas the previous definition sets the concept of gatekeeping squarely within the political realm by discussing struggles of power, resources, and opportunities, this definition refers to access and rights within communities and identities. The Urban Dictionary definition of gatekeeping opens up the realm of gatekeeping beyond the political, and suggests that gatekeeping can also occur in cultural and community-based circumstances. Of course, gatekeeping at its core can occur in many situations, and shouldn't be limited to the political sphere, but focusing more on the community sphere than the political sphere in this definition is a definitive choice, and a slightly more modern one than is represented in the definition from the Cambridge Dictionary.

The final definition we will consider under the umbrella of gatekeeping is the definition of a gatekeeper. According to Dictionary.com, a gatekeeper is "a person or thing that controls access to, as to information, often acting as an arbiter of quality or legitimacy" (2021). Now, it's important that we consider the definitions of both gatekeeping and gatekeeper, as there are key clues in both definitions that lead to a broader understanding of the concept of gatekeeping. As noted in the Dictionary.com definition, gatekeepers aren't just controlling access; they are also creating the standards of what people can expect to receive.
What exactly does that mean?

Most readers here will recognize the title of the famous children's book *Goodnight Moon*, which was included in an addendum to the list of the top ten most borrowed books from the New York Public Library (NYPL). The list, which celebrated the NYPL's 125th anniversary, notes that *Goodnight Moon* was extraordinarily popular, and without question would have made and even topped the list - except for one problem: "influential New York Public Library children's librarian Anne Carroll Moore disliked the story so much when it was published in 1947 that the Library didn't carry it …

until 1972" (Kois, 2020). Let's take a quick dive into this story so we can establish exactly what this one children's librarian had against *Goodnight Moon*, and why she managed to keep it out of the NYPL for 25 years.

Anne Carroll Moore represented a shift in focus for the NYPL; in fact, before she joined the NYPL as the first 'superintendent of work with children,' children weren't encouraged to be in libraries. After all, what would children do in a library when they were only learning to read? Moore took her job seriously, and found numerous ways to create a welcome space in the library for these children, including story hours and offering them the option to sign out their own books. With this view in mind, Moore was doing a great thing: sharing the power of reading with a generation that hadn't been welcomed into libraries before.

Moore's groundbreaking work put her in a position that other libraries watched closely. They watched which books the NYPL purchased, and more importantly, which books they didn't purchase. Leonard Marcus noted that:

> If Anne Carroll Moore didn't like a book, she could effectively kill it. Editors, authors, and illustrators routinely stopped by to visit with Miss Moore and seek her counsel on their works in progress; she supposedly had a custom-made rubber stamp reading "NOT RECOMMENDED FOR PURCHASE BY EXPERT," and she was not afraid to use it (Marcus, quoted in Kois, 2020).

Now, let's take a moment to note that this position of power made Anne Carroll Moore the ultimate gatekeeper for children's literature. Based on her own thoughts and beliefs about what was best for children, she was effectively selecting which books were and weren't going to reach children's hands, which had a tremendous impact on the books overall. Moore was able to effectively kill books, like Marcus noted, because if she stamped that book saying that it was not recommended for purchase, other libraries would follow her lead and also not buy the book. In some cases, this could lead the book to flop entirely, because it wouldn't have a market for purchase - all because one woman decided she didn't think it was worthy for reading by children.

Goodnight Moon was one of those books that Anne Carroll Moore found to be distasteful for children, and used her infamous stamp on. Even though Moore was halfway out the door to retirement by the time *Goodnight Moon* came across her desk, she still held that fundamental position of power which allowed her to crush books where they stood. It didn't matter how much effort the authors of these books put in to impress Anne Carroll Moore - if she didn't like a book, it wasn't going into circulation.

Margaret Wise Brown wanted librarians to adopt *Goodnight Moon*; she even blurred out the udder of the cow who jumped over the moon to avoid offending those "Important Ladies." But it certainly wasn't enough for Moore, or Sayers, or the NYPL: Marcus notes that "in a harshly worded internal review, the library dismissed the book as an unbearably sentimental piece of work." And so the book wasn't purchased by the New York Public Library, and while children were encouraged to check out all kinds of books from the library's extensive children's department, *Goodnight Moon* was not one of them (Mois, 2020).

Anne Carroll Moore is a perfect example of a gatekeeper, and gatekeeping in practice. In a certain circumstance - that of children's books and the NYPL - she decided which books merited reaching the hands of children, and which books should remain hidden from them. Her gatekeeping impacted not only the children to whom she was providing and gatekeeping books from - it also impacted the authors whose books were and weren't provided to children, and the overall children's literature sector. Though the authors of this book could talk about Anne Carroll Moore and the impacts of her gatekeeping for much longer than this short overview, it's time for us to move on to look at the second definition we're exploring in this section: censorship.

The Cambridge Dictionary defines censorship as "the action of preventing part or the whole of a book, film, work of art, document, or other kind of communication from being seen or made available to the public, because it is considered to be offensive or harmful, or because it contains information that someone wishes to keep secret, often for political reasons" (2021). Now, this might sound like gatekeeping, in that it focuses on the limiting of ideas that people can express, but the key difference is the purpose of the keeping of the gates. As this definition of censorship notes, censorship's focus is on ensuring that the information provided focuses only on the viewpoint that the censors want it to. We'll look at the functional similarities and differences between censorship and gatekeeping after we look at two other definitions of censorship.

Merriam-Webster defines a censor as: "a person who supervises conduct and morals: such as a: an official who examines materials (such as publications or films) for objectionable matter; for example, a. Government censors deleted all references to the protest, or b: an official (as in time of war) who reads communications (such as letters) and deletes material considered sensitive or harmful" (Merriam-Webster, 2021). Again in this definition, the focus becomes on the conduct and morals portrayed within a specific form of media. Think about any spy movie who has requested information from the government, but their request returns a redacted file that sees three quarters of the words blacked out. That is an excellent example of censorship, and fits well into this definition of a censor.

The Encyclopaedia Britannica defines censorship as "the changing or the suppression or prohibition of speech or writing that is deemed subversive of the common good. It occurs in all manifestations of authority to some degree, but in modern times it has been of special importance in its relation to government and the rule of law" (Anastaplo, 2020). This definition takes us a step further from just suppression and prohibition of certain focuses and topics, and suggests that physically changing information can be a form of censorship. The focus here on government and rule of law is also prevalent, and is something we will discuss in relation to the Canadian government when we reach chapter three.

Now that we've had a chance to explore differing definitions between censorship and gatekeeping, it's time to really clearly lay out the differences between the two, because though their definitions sound similar in practice, they actually represent two very different kinds of information protection. For the purposes of this book, the realm of gatekeeping exists within the decision-making and decision-makers regarding the publication or sharing of information, regardless of the reason. Censorship lives more within the political realm, and is focused more on what information isn't provided, than the information that is. The key difference between gatekeeping and censorship, then, lives within the focus: gatekeeping is focused on what is shared, and censorship is focused on what *isn't* shared. Let's add propaganda into the mix, now, and understand how it differs from and is similar to, gatekeeping and censorship.

Merriam-Webster defines propaganda as "the spreading of ideas, information, or rumor for the purpose of helping or injuring an institution, a cause, or a person" (Merriam-Webster, 2021). Propaganda, then, is less focused on the actual keeping of the gates in regards to what information gets out; instead, its focus is on spreading information that has a specific lens on a certain idea or topic. Even when it comes to censorship, only one definition suggested that censorship constituted spreading information that was inaccurate, so propaganda functions very differently from gatekeeping, and fairly differently from censorship as well.

The Encyclopaedia Britannica asserts that propaganda is: "dissemination of information—facts, arguments, rumours, half-truths, or lies—to influence public opinion" (Smith, 2021). Just like the last definition noted, propaganda focuses on sharing specific information that influences public opinion in one specific way. We'll be learning about propaganda when we talk about John Grierson in section two, but again, it's important to note that where gatekeeping and censorship are focused on what is and isn't shared, propaganda is focused on sharing information that meets their specific agenda. Consider COVID-19 - there are plenty of people that are sharing propaganda that attempts to debunk the efficacy of the vaccine. Since we know that the vaccine has been scientifically proven as effective, we know that any information that attempts to debunk the vaccine can be labelled as propaganda because it isn't true.

The final definition of propaganda that we will consider in this section is from the Cambridge Dictionary, which defines propaganda as: information, ideas, opinions, or images, often only giving one part of an argument, that are broadcast, published, or in some other way spread with the intention of influencing people's opinions" (Cambridge Dictionary, 2021). This definition includes a note that propaganda is often used in arguments, and often only broadcast one side of said argument.

It's important for us to remember that anything deemed propaganda is not providing two sides of an argument, and certainly isn't providing information that the opposing side would agree with. Propaganda's specific focus is to change the minds of the people reading or listening to propagandistic material, regardless of the cost.

Now, we looked at an example of gatekeeping when we talked about Anne Carroll Moore and *Goodnight Moon*, which helped us understand exactly how the realm of a gatekeeper works. When we talked about censorship, we referenced the ways in which some government organizations will redact information about, for example, military operations - focusing on the information that isn't provided. We will discuss propaganda in detail when we talk about John Grierson, but as we know, the names Adolf Hitler and Joseph Gobbels are the most well known when it comes to propaganda because of the extensive propaganda campaign they ran during Nazi Germany to convince Germans to turn against their Jewish neighbours and friends. With these examples in mind, let's set out a clear distinction between the three phrases, before we move into a discussion about print media.

The biggest difference between the three terms - gatekeeping, censorship, and propaganda - can be found in their focus. Gatekeeping focuses on the information that is provided. Censorship focuses on the information that is not provided, by choosing what information to provide to meet an agenda. Propaganda focuses on providing information that proves a point, whether it is accurate or not. By understanding the difference in focus between these three terms, we can understand why this book focuses on gatekeeping, and not censorship or propaganda. Much of the conversations we will have within this book focus on gatekeeping because we want to consider what is provided to us, and within that consideration, what is missing from our offerings and why it might not have made the cut.

Now that we've taken the time to explore gatekeeping, censorship, and propaganda, and understand exactly why this book focuses on gatekeeping more so than censorship and propaganda, it's time for us to dive into the 'meat and potatoes' of our discussion. We'll now be moving into our two main explorations: print media and digital media. The print media section will focus on Canadian communication theorists and theories in relation to print media, while the digital media section will be more focused on the actual media and the ways in which they are gatekept within Canada and Canadian rules and laws. Finally, we'll briefly discuss the ethics in gatekeeping, before concluding with the question: how do we find and consider gatekeeping within our own lives? Without further ado, let's jump into print media, gatekeeping, and Canadian communication theory and media.

Chapter 2:
Print Media

Print media is a particularly fascinating facet of gatekeeping within Canadian media, and exploring gatekeeping and print media through the lenses of various communication theorists will provide us with a deep and thorough understanding of exactly how gatekeeping in print media differs from and is similar to the upcoming discussion on digital media. This section will be built upon theorists: we'll begin with a brief introduction to each theorist, which will provide us with the context necessary to understand their unique perspectives and theories. From there, we will explore one or two specific examples of the ways in which each theorist would view and address gatekeeping in print media. Finally, we'll compare and contrast the ways in which each theorist would consider our examples, to ensure we have a well-rounded understanding of each theory. We can't begin, of course, without understanding exactly what we mean when we say 'print media,' so our initial section will be, in part, a definition and exploration of print media, and in second part, be an explanation of why we chose to consider certain print media sources and not others.

What is Print Media?

Before we begin to dive into this chapter, it's important for us to take a moment and explore exactly what's meant by the phrase 'print media.' Print media is one of those phrases that people think they understand, though because there are varying understandings of the phrase across literature and study, it can be confusing if an author doesn't define their terms to ensure that the author(s) and reader(s) are on the same page. We'll begin our exploration of print media by looking at the two phrases individually, before putting them together and providing some examples of what we authors mean, in this book, when we refer to print media.

Media is a particularly curious word, as it has grown in definition and use since its original addition to the English vernacular. Nowadays, most readers would liken media to news media before they would consider any other definition of the phrase. Because of this fact, let's take some time to explore exactly what we mean when the authors of this book refer to the phrase 'media.' To begin, we need to understand that we are using media as a plural noun, which means that the noun in question is actually medium.

Chances are everyone reading this book has heard the phrase 'the medium is the message,' coined by Canadian communication theorist Marshall McLuhan, who we will be discussing shortly. When McLuhan refers to a medium, he is speaking of "a means of effecting or conveying something" (Merriam-Webster, 2021). In essence, the medium is the way in which a message is transmitted. Media, being the plural of medium, then refers to the multiple of a medium, or multiple transmission methods. Though the phrase 'media' has become synonymous in this day and age with news media and media outlets, it's important to remember that in the case of this book, if the authors are specifically referring to news media, we will specify 'news media.' Otherwise, our references to media and a medium are completely in line with the definitions noted above. Making this distinction is important, because without this context, the topic of conversation could be very confusing to a reader if they think we are utilizing one connotation of the word when we are actually using another.

Similarly, when we refer to print media, we are referring to a specific subsection of media - transmission methods - that are transmitted via printed materials. Now, there are hundreds of different definitions of print media, ranging in limitation from referring only to newspapers and magazines to referring to anything that is or can be printed, including online articles and this book in a PDF form. For the purposes of this book, when the authors refer to print media, we are referring to media that is presented to the reader in a printed or printable form. Included in this definition is everything from the physical book in your hand, the piece of paper that you scribbled your grocery list on, the newspaper sitting in your mailbox, and yes, the PDF copy of this book that you may or may not be reading on your computer or e-reader.

Now that we have a clear understanding of what print media is, and what fits within the definition of print media, it's time for us to jump into the communication theorists, theories, and examples that we are going to discuss, to help us better understand the conversations surrounding gatekeeping within Canadian media. We will address theorists in no particular order, though some theories are reflected in others, so there is some semblance of logic in the order through which we introduce you to theorists and theories. To begin, we'll learn about Harold Adams Innis, and his staple theory which is - dare we say it - a staple to our understanding of the remainder of all communication theorists and theories we will discuss in this book.

Through the Lens: Harold Adams Innis

It's difficult to talk about Canadian communication theory without speaking about Harold Adams Innis. Innis's 'staple thesis' is - dare we say it again - a staple within Canadian communication theory, and sparks fascinating discussion and ideas around exactly why Canadian communication theory exists differently than other communication theories around the world. It is sensible, then, that we discuss Harold Adams Innis very first, because the way in which we consider the remainder of the communication theorists in this section and in the rest of the book should be with Innis's theories and ideas in mind.

Let's begin, then, with some context: who exactly was Harold Adams Innis, and why is he important to Canadian communication theory? He must have been important, seeing as the Library and Archives of Canada notes Innis to be "one of the most influential academics Canada has ever produced" (2018). Well, Harold Adams Innis was born in Ontario on November 5, 1894, in southern Ontario. He grew up in a religious family, and his mother was hoping that Innis would join the church as a minister in his adult life. Instead of joining the church, Innis went to post-secondary education, following his grade school learnings in a single-room schoolhouse, and received a Bachelor of Arts in history and political economy at McMaster University (Babe, 2014, p. 52).

Following his achievement of his Bachelor's degree, Innis signed up to join the military to support Canada in WWI. After completing basic training, Innis wanted to go overseas. As Library and Archives Canada notes:

[Innis] enlisted with the 69th Overseas Battery, Canadian Field Artillery, on May 17, 1916. He arrived in France on November 16, 1916, and served there until he was wounded by shrapnel in the right thigh at Vimy Ridge on July 7, 1917. As a result of this wound, he was sent back to Canada on March 16, 1918 (Library and Archives Canada, 2018).

Upon Innis's return, he elected to continue his education, and went on to achieve a Masters of Arts, completing a thesis titled "The Returned Soldier" (Babe, 2014, p. 52). From there, he went on to receive his doctorate in political economy from the University of Chicago. He returned to Canada in 1920, when he was appointed to "the Department of Political Economy at the University of Toronto, where he served as chair from 1937 until his death in 1952 (Babe, 2014, p. 53). Interestingly, though Innis went through a remarkable amount of schooling, he preferred any means of communication rather than that of written communication. According to Robert Babe:

Innis expressed disdain for most written communication. Written texts, he pointed out, customarily lead readers through their authors' sequence of reasoning to preconceived conclusions, rather than opening up new possibilities and raising new questions for readers. He mused: 'The most dangerous illusions accompany the most obvious facts including the printed and mechanical word' (Babe, 2014, p. 57).

Written communication, like any form of communication, has its faults, and it's important to remember that though Innis noted the flaws of written communication, it was a form he utilized again and again, partly from necessity, and partly from a desire to offer the opportunity for his readers to find new possibilities and questions from the writing he provided them. Innis presented some of his best and most recognized works in the written form, and it is here in another written form where we will explore his concepts and their applications to our world. From there, we will better be able to understand exactly how Innis considered gatekeeping within the realm of Canadian media.

Now, in order for us to understand Innis's thought process, there are two aspects of his theories that we need to understand. We need to understand his thoughts on media as communication, and how media are entrenched in and so reflective of a specific community. Then, we need to understand how he connected economics, staples, and communication to demonstrate the ways in which communication can be dependent on staples, and therefore the economics and technology utilized in growing, harvesting, and selling the staples. Within each aspect, we will consider an example of how Innis's thought can be put into practice, to ensure that our understanding of his theories is as practical and applicable as possible.

We'll begin by exploring the reasons why Innis equated the Canadian Pacific Railway as a method of communication within Canada. In some ways, it is obvious: the railway permitted long-distance communication to travel much more quickly than other methods at that time, and shared various types of communication - written, verbal, and more. As Robert Babe explains, Innis considered communication media in three ways:

1. Technologies, or ways of doing things, arise *from* civilizations, and hence they manifest the prototypical concerns and thought patterns of the particular society.

2. Technologies *have an impact* upon civilizations and thus are key to understanding a civilization's evolution.

3. Technologies are the *means* (i.e., the media) whereby civilizations spread and contact one another (Babe, 2014, p. 61).

Based on these three concepts, we can logically understand why Innis would consider the railway to be a form of communication media. If he considered the railway in this way, let us take a moment to consider another technology: the airplane. Airplane travel is much more common now than it was in Innis's day, and the reasoning for this form of travel becoming more common is because our society has evolved to offer and require faster modes of transportation across large distances. In that way, airplanes manifest the concerns of our society - a need to create a network of quick opportunities to travel globally - and our thought patterns. Of course, airplane travel has had a tremendous impact upon our society, and has played an important part in our evolution. We've become so used to being able to hop on a plane for a meeting in another country, to go on vacation somewhere sunny, or even to fly home to visit family for the winter holidays. And finally, there's no question that airplane travel has led to our civilization spreading and contacting one another. In that way, we can understand why Innis considers the Canadian Pacific Railway, and would likely now consider airplanes, to be forms of communication.

Now that we have explored one aspect of Innis's communication thought, it's time to explore one of his most popular theories: the staple thesis. The thesis, or theory, explores and attempts to explain why Canada developed as it did, in terms of economics, exploration, communication, and much more. According to Innis, the staple commodities that Canada hosts played a significant part in the ways in which it grew, and the reasons why it grew in those particular ways. In general:

> Innis's staple theory narrative, fleshed out in the 1930s and 1940s, is deeply imbedded [sic] in a detailed discourse of Canadian economic history, wherein Canadian economic evolution and development is explained through highly detailed historical analyses of the development of key commodities such as cod, furs, timber, and the transportation infrastructure which allowed for and facilitated the export of such products (Encyclopedia.com, 2021).

Innis's staple thesis, like many communication theories, transcends the barriers between disciplines, and has been referenced as both an economic theory and a communication theory. That said, since our prime focus is on communication and not economics, we are going to lean more on the communication side of Innis's theory. For that reason, even though Innis never formally wrote on lumber as a staple like he did fish and fur, we are going to explore Canada's connection to the lumber and forestry staple, and how that impacted the writing and publishing industry in Canada and beyond. From there, we will be able to explore how the physical availability of materials impacts gatekeeping and selections of what is publishable, when things are published, and why.

Let's begin by remembering the importance of timber and the timber industry. If you look around you right now, a number of things in your vicinity will have been born from timber. Your kitchen table is likely wooden, or at least parts of it are. The building you're living in or working from will have been constructed from wood. The books on your bookshelf originated as timber. The chair or couch you are sitting on likely has a wooden frame or other wooden aspects. So much of our everyday lives depend on the timber industry, just as people did during Innis's time.

As we discussed early on in this book, Canada is known for its vast, nature-filled landscape, and a major portion of that landscape consists of trees. For this reason, the timber industry became popular in Canada, because there was an abundance of resources available for the picking. Now, you might be thinking: Canada has many more resources than just trees - there's fur and fish and so many other staples existing. That is important to note, because there's something that differs the timber trade from any other trade, and that's the size of the material when it's ready to be shipped. Fur and fish are reasonably small, but timber requires much more effort to transport, particularly in the form of chopped-down trees. For this reason, timber was manufactured in Canada, more often than not, so it was lumber, instead of timber, that was being shipped out. Of course, manufacturing creates jobs, bringing in new workers, and feeding the economy of a town with a timber factory. That, Innis believed, was critical to the staple theory.

Now, let's think about paper, instead of lumber and timber. Paper is one of the most common media that are used for communication, which makes paper a fairly hot commodity. Being able to turn timber into pulp into paper was key for early Canada, because it meant that Canada could take the big bulky timber and make it into a much-needed commodity that was far easier to pack and ship than a bunch of massive logs. The availability of timber and paper, then, is a major factor within gatekeeping. If there is an abundance or shortage of paper available to print books, for example, then the decision-making process for what books are printed, what books aren't printed, and how many copies of books are printed becomes either easier or more complicated.

It's important to think about just how influential paper and the paper industry is, and to remember what disdain Innis had for written communication as a whole. Innis is quoted as saying:

Expansion of the pulp and paper industry has supported intensive advertising and revolutions in marketing essential to the demands of the city. It has coincided with the decline of editorials and of freedom of speech, and the emergence of headlines and the modern newspaper with its demands for excitement, including wars and peace, to appeal to a large range of lower mental types" (Innis, quoted in Babe, 2014, p. 69).

While Innis recognizes the importance and modernity of paper and written communication, it's clear that he feels that written communication, newspapers in particular, aren't focused on the more intellectual people in society. When we learn about John Grierson in a later section, we can compare Innis's thoughts on mass communication and it's audience to Grierson's, and his thoughts on how information should be shared with the general public to ensure it is understood and appreciated in the ways it is intended.

Now, books aren't the only media of import when it comes to paper. Again, with recognition of Innis's disdain for written communication in mind, he did note and study the importance of which newspapers had within society. As Robert Babe notes, "newspapers played a large role in transforming the conception of time - from continuity to sequential uniformity - and as well the conception of space - from one concerning locality where community resides, to borderless geographic extent organized through principals of commodity exchange" (Babe, 2014, p. 69 - 70). Printed newspapers were a staple in most homes across North America and beyond before computers, and it was a daily ritual to drink one's coffee while sitting on the porch or at the kitchen table and reading the newspaper. Can you imagine the outrage if the newspaper hadn't been on the porch one morning?

If we think closely about it, the decision not to print or deliver a newspaper is a form of gatekeeping. Regardless of the reason, even if it is due to a paper shortage, the physical act of not providing a piece of information to the public is a form of gatekeeping. Newspapers carry vital news, and in Innis's day when people couldn't count on the internet or Twitter for their news, those newspapers were one of the only ways that people received their news. How were they to know what was going on in the world if not to read it in the newspaper? Of course, there were other ways of receiving information, but it's important to recognize the cultural significance of the newspaper, and how it impacts and impacted people's lives.

Though Innis didn't theorize about gatekeeping specifically, his theories take us into territory that is often unexplored when it comes to the keeping of the gates. If we consider the supply chain of media and communication materials, we recognize that not all gatekeeping decisions are made after a material is prepared and ready; in some cases, that decision is made long before the material is even in a full form. By recognizing this fact, we are understanding that there is no one way that gatekeeping is accomplished. In some cases, a lack of materials requires people in high places to make difficult decisions about what goes to print and what lays on the newsroom floor. Is this gatekeeping? By definition, yes it is. In practice, gatekeeping examples like this are often forgotten in favour of examples where it's a strategic choice to publish one article and withhold the other, in cases where supply is not a factor.

Innis's theories spanned more widely than what is reflected in these pages, yet what we've done here is distilled the essence of his theories and understandings so that we could explore his theories in the context of gatekeeping, and the ways in which supply and demand, staples, and more impact whether or not a product reaches its recipients hands. We will keep this exploration in mind as we move forward to consider our next communication theorist and the unique way in which he considers communication theory, gatekeeping, and Canadian media.

Through the Lens: Marshall McLuhan

Marshall McLuhan is one of the most well-known and well-recognized names in global and Canadian communication theory. His saying "the medium is the message" is known across the globe, and has been the basis of many theories and studies. Though he did not speak directly to gatekeeping within his various theories, an exploration into his thought process demonstrates that he inadvertently was discussing gatekeeping, in his own way. Let's explore McLuhan's life, before we begin to unpack one of his most popular and well-known theories.

Marshall McLuhan was born in Edmonton, Alberta, on July 21, 1911. His mother was a stage performer and a schoolteacher, and his father was a real estate agent. McLuhan took after his mother, who encouraged him to read from an early age, leading to his interest in academics. Though McLuhan was born in Edmonton, he grew up in Winnipeg, where he became interested in radio broadcasting, which was in its formative years, and in religion; in fact, while studying at the University of Manitoba, McLuhan converted to Catholicism. McLuhan started his university career in engineering, but it only took a year before he switched to arts, with a focus on English, history, and philosophy (Babe, 2014, p. 267). After receiving a BA and an MA in arts at the University of Winnipeg, he moved to Cambridge University, where he enrolled as an undergraduate, and then to the University of Wisconsin, where he was hired as a graduate teaching assistant. After moving between Cambridge, where he received his PhD, and Windsor, where he taught, "he moved to St. Michael's College at the University of Toronto, whereupon he wrote to his friend and former student Walter Ong: 'So Walter, I must regard this move as a permanent one.' And so it proved" (Babe, 2014, p. 269).

Important to note is that McLuhan studied the works of Harold Adams Innis, in fact, "McLuhan often referred to himself as being a 'disciple of Harold Adams Innis'" (Babe, 2014, p. 273). Since we have already explored a section of Innis's studies, it is important for us to remember that McLuhan saw his work as building upon that of what Innis had started. Possibly the most important connection between Harold Adams Innis and Marshall McLuhan is the fact that "McLuhan accepted wholeheartedly Innis's main thesis that culture, society, and civilization change in tandem with changes in the media of communication" (Babe, 2014, p. 274). With this fact in mind, let's take a moment to explore McLuhan's most popular theory: the medium is the message.

Of course, it would be remiss of us to begin to explore McLuhan's theory without first taking the time to understand his definition of media and medium. According to McLuhan, media is a "generic term for all human-invented technology that extends the range, speed, or channels of communication" (Griffin et al., 2015, p. 317), and a medium is "a specific type of media for example, a book, newspaper, radio, television, telephone, film, website, or email" (Griffin et al., 2015, p. 317). With his aphorism "the medium is the message," then, McLuhan is suggesting that the channel delivering the message plays a significant part in how the message is interpreted. Communication scholars Em Griffin, Andrew Ledbetter, and Glenn Sparks, explain:

We focus on the content and overlook the *medium* - even though content doesn't exist outside of the way it's mediated. *Moby Dick* is a book. *Moby Dick* is a movie. *Moby Dick* is an oral tale. These are different stories. For this reason, we shouldn't complain that a movie is not like a book, because a movie can never be like a book. A movie can only be a movie (Griffin et al., 2015, p. 317).

Now, this example can be a bit polarizing to those who firmly believe that books can be properly (and so, improperly) reflected within films. After all, we've all seen a movie that reflects a book really well, and we've also seen an unfortunate film that looks nothing like the book it is originally based on. That said, the key to this example is the idea that the medium plays a fundamental part in the way in which a message is understood. The message doesn't exist separate from the medium, and so they are intertwined: the medium doesn't exist without the message, and the message doesn't exist without the medium.

Let's take a moment and consider an example of this concept in work. Let's say that you want to send a message to one of your friends and let them know that something they said about you last night really hurt your feelings. You have a few options as to how to have that conversation with them: you could send a text, call them, or get together in-person. Of course, there are benefits and detriments to each and all of your options. On one hand, sending a text means that the conversation will be less awkward, because you will have more time to craft and perfect your message before sending it, and your friend has time to consider what you've said before replying. On the other hand, sending a text denies both you and your friend the opportunity to see the context provided by body language and voice that would be helpful in deciphering the tone and general vibe of the message. Your friend could think you're kidding, over text, because they aren't able to hear it in your voice that you are actually hurt. Though they could get that impression over the phone, they would still be missing the body language markers that would only be present within an in-person conversation.

Of course, we could analyze examples like this all day, but when it comes down to it, we need to understand that the medium through which we share a message is intrinsically tied to the way in which the message is perceived and understood. We know that texting is difficult sometimes because the person on the receiving end of the text isn't able to decipher the tone of the text because they simply don't have enough contextual information to be able to tell. This fact leads into what McLuhan referred to as the global village: "a worldwide electronic community where everyone knows everyone's business and all are somewhat testy" (Griffin et al., 2015, p. 321). The best way to understand the concept of a global village is to think about Facebook. Facebook is a worldwide electronic community, where people share (and often overshare) information about their lives. Though in many cases, Facebook can be supportive of people having a baby or getting a new job, Facebook is also a breeding ground for anger and cyber-bullying. Twitter is another excellent example of a global village, though we suspect that when McLuhan was writing about the global village, he was referring to society as a whole. Because we are all consistently connected through various types of digital media like video calling, social media, and the internet, everyone inherently knows everyone's business, and there's no question that people are remarkably testy, especially when they are glued to their devices and feel unable to take the time to experience the world around them.

Now, inherent within all of McLuhan's communication thought was the understanding that politics factored into communication, media, and messages - sometimes intentionally, and sometimes without the recipient's understanding. McLuhan believed that:

The true artist, [McLuhan] contented, like the inventor, is the 'ultimate enemy' or established power. The artist causes perfections to change, thereby enabling people to see things as they really are. Similarly inventors create products and processes that, by transforming environments, increase awareness. Awareness, for McLuhan, is always an enemy of established power (Babe, 2014, p. 293).

What does this mean, for gatekeeping, then? Well, let's consider what constitutes an artist, and how artists play into gatekeeping. In an ideal world, an author would be considered an artist, because their purpose is to enable people to see things as they really are. When we talk about Gertrude Joch Robinson and her theory of truth, we will discuss the concept of truth further, but it's not difficult for us to recognize that each and every person in this world has some form of bias, whether conscious or unconscious, that would come across in their writing. Everyone sees the world in a unique way, and before we can consider how people help others 'see things as they really are,' we have to consider how we define the natural state of things, since they differ by individual.

That said, McLuhan's concept that the artist causes perfections to change is particularly interesting, because it is arguable that the purpose of the gatekeeper is to keep the image of perfection, and the artist to find a way past the gatekeeper and share the truth of the matter, so that audiences can understand exactly how the world is existing. We know that there are people in this world who believe that the Holocaust was a hoax. If they were functioning as the gatekeeper, they would be attempting to keep materials proving the Holocaust from a specific audience, be it their classroom, their children, or their family. To them, the materials proving that the Holocaust existed and happened are untrue and fake. They believe that it falls to them, then, to ensure that the real truth - that the Holocaust was a hoax - is shared within their circles. On the other hand, the people that know that the Holocaust was a real, terrible event, share materials that prove its truth, and try to suppress the materials that attempt to disprove the Holocaust. They know that the truth is that the Holocaust happened, and want to ensure that the information they share is proving the actual truth.

When we consider this example, we realize that gatekeeping exists in blurry circumstances. The question of truth and reality circles the way in which the gates are kept, and it's the gatekeeper's version of truth that is either proven or disproven based on what the gatekeeper shares with the general public. Consider children's books, for example. In the previous chapter, we were introduced to a New York librarian that successfully blacklisted a children's book simply because she disliked the story. How do we know that a similar sort of gatekeeping isn't occurring in children's literature right now? Is it happening at a parent level, where the parents have the choice of what to provide their children, or is happening at a higher level, where the parents think they have a choice of what to provide their children based on what is available at bookstores, but really their choices are limited by what's actually published?

This ethical issue will be explored further in a later chapter, but it's important to note that McLuhan had this concept in mind as he was exploring communication thought. Between his understanding of gatekeeping and political economy and his focus on the medium and the message, he may not have studied gatekeeping outright, but his communication thought expressed important questions regarding information: how it was received, how it was sent, and what meaning is imbued to the message based on the medium through which it was sent. Let's consider one final example of McLuhan's work and gatekeeping before we move on to our next communication theorist.

If, in fact, the medium is the message, then let's consider the way in which messages differ when provided from two different forms of print media: a newspaper and a book. If we were reading about a historical event, for example, the ways in which we perceive that event would be different based simply upon the medium in which we take in the information. Before many of them went digital, newspapers were a staple in the household: nearly everyone can remember a father, a grandfather, or even yourself sitting down, coffee in hand, and opening the newspaper. Not only do print newspapers have a specific cultural purpose, but they also have a specific form that readers expect when they open them. Articles are reasonably short (compared to the length of a book), meaning that they are required to omit certain details for the sake of being succinct. Additionally, most newspapers are connected to some form of a political stance or angle, meaning that the journalist writing the article will often be spinning the story in a specific way; not telling lies, but utilizing specific facts to draw the reader to a specific conclusion. Now, that's not to say that every journalist and every article has a specific angle and that nothing you read in the news is actually true; instead, it's a reminder that when you take in any media, it's important to consider where the message is coming from and how that might impact your interpretation of said media.

Books, on the other hand, are a long form of writing: chances are high that there will be more detail and more story within a book, simply due to the length of the form. Non-fiction books in particular will take time to delve into interesting facts and details where newspapers will have to cut those facts out due to spacing issues. While newspapers typically found their cultural place on the porch or at the kitchen table, books exist anywhere and anywhere, and are often preferred when a person wants to sit down and read for an extended period of time, instead of for a short while.

Of course, the authors of said books, like journalists, will inevitably be attempting to prove a thesis, argue a point, or generally attempt to ensure that the reader will walk away from the book with a specific understanding in mind. As we discussed earlier, the question of truth will be considered by a later theorist, but it is important to remember that since the medium impacts the message, the way we consider a message should be in relation to the medium through which it was presented to us.

As with all of the communication theorists we discuss in this section, there is much more to Marshall McLuhan's communication thought than just what we have covered here. That said, considering McLuhan's theories with the lens of gatekeeping has led us to some important understanding about the way in which a message is presented, and how gatekeeping can inherently factor into the message. In addition, we opened discussion of truth and focus of the authors of messages - a discussion which we will continue later in this section. For now, it's time to say farewell to Marshall McLuhan's communication thought, and move towards the thought of another fascinating communication theorist: John Grierson.

Through the Lens: John Grierson

Though John Grierson's focus throughout his career as a Canadian communication theorist was predominantly on digital media and documentary film, it would be remiss of the authors of this book not to introduce him and explore some of his theories in relation to print media in advance of discussing his focus on documentary film. Of course, as with the previous theorists we've discussed, it's time for us to take a quick dive into the life and works of John Grierson before we begin to explore his theories and how they impact gatekeeping and print media.

John Grierson was not born in Canada, nor did he grow up in Canada. Grierson was born near Doune, Scotland, on April 26, 1898. His father was a schoolmaster, and his mother was a teacher. It makes sense, then, that Grierson was brought up believing in the importance of education, learning, and information sharing for the betterment of society. When WWI began, Grierson wanted nothing more than to fight for his country, and did so by becoming a telegraphist - apt, considering his upbringing. When the war ended, Grierson returned to his love for education, and studied English literature and philosophy at the University of Glasgow. It was after he graduated, and when he was lecturing in the United States of America, that Grierson met the men who would help guide him on his path to creating meaningful change around the world, as it came to education. Walter Lippmann, political writer, and Robert Flaherty, documentary filmmaker, had an enormous impact on the future of Grierson's career, though none of the men knew it when they first met.

As Robert Babe notes, "Grierson interviewed Lippmann, who advised the aspiring journalist to forsake press studies and investigate instead the educational possibilities of the cinema, guidance that caused Grierson soon to visit Hollywood and Paramount Pictures" (2014, p. 90). This visit to Hollywood and Paramount Pictures introduced Grierson to the work of Robert Flaherty, which opened Grierson's eyes to the power and truth that existed within documentary film. After some thought and experience considering films and documentary films, Grierson found his path: "to use the cinema to touch as many people as possible with the democratic ideal" (Babe, 2014, p. 91). As Robert Babe notes:

> Flaherty's pioneering work notwithstanding, the concept of *documentary* film was practically invented by Grierson. He variously defined documentary as 'the creative treatment of actuality,' as film 'made from natural material,' and as the cinematic presentation of 'drama that resides in the living fact.' He chose *film* as his principal medium because it enabled him to reach a wide audience. And he selected *documentary* film because, he said, it is 'closer to the people and events' (Babe, 2014, p. 91.

Of course, once Grierson found his place in communication theory, there he stood, and from there he rose. We will cover his exploits and successes within documentary film when we speak about documentary film in the next section. For now, it's time for us to take some time to explore why documentary film called to him specifically, and the ways in which he considered the ethics of propaganda within art and democracy. We will then apply his theories to a practical, print-based example, which will help us better understand his truly fascinating take on democratic propaganda.

The first theory, or concept, of Grierson's that we will explore is that of democratic propaganda. Now, the phrase 'propaganda' is much like 'censorship' and 'gatekeeping:' everyone either thinks they know what it means, or has heard it used enough times that they feel comfortable guessing about its definition. For that reason, to ensure that we have an open mind and no preconceived notions about what propaganda is as we go into this section of Grierson's work, we are going to take a moment here and explore the etymology and history of the term 'propaganda' before we continue exploring the concept of democratic propaganda. Though we did discuss propaganda in the introduction, it's worth refreshing ourselves on exactly what constitutes propaganda and how it fits within Grierson's thought.

The Encyclopaedia Britannica defines propaganda as "the more or less systematic effort to manipulate other people's beliefs, attitudes, or actions by means of symbols (words, gestures, banners, monuments, music, clothing, insignia, hairstyles, designs on coins and postage stamps, and so forth" (Smith, 2021). In essence, then, propaganda is a form of persuasion, with the intent on ensuring the audience of the propaganda forms a specific opinion of a person, place, or thing. The most common place in which the phrase 'propaganda' is utilized is when discussing politics and political rules; most often, that of Adolf Hitler. As most of you likely already knew, Hitler, and his associate Joseph Gobbels, were masterful propagandists, and utilized their skills to strengthen the Nazi party and push their anger towards the Jewish community, as well as other marginalized communities in Germany.

In regards to propaganda, Hitler believed that the: "task is not to make an objective study of the truth, in so far as it favors the enemy, and then set it before the masses with academic fairness; its task is to serve our own right, always and unflinchingly" (United States Holocaust Memorial Museum, 2021). In Hitler's view, propaganda's purpose was to share *their* truth, not the objective truth. This idea of truth is a concept that we will discuss and study when we speak about Canadian communication theorist Gertrude Joch Robinson, but for now, we need to understand that when propaganda is referenced, it is referring to sharing one truth, not the objective truth. This is different from gatekeeping, because where gatekeeping prevents information from being released, propaganda's purpose is spreading information (or misinformation) that is intended to shape other people's beliefs, attitudes, or actions in a specific and often systemic way.

It's important to note that when Grierson was using the word 'propaganda,' it had a very different context and connotation than it does for those of us that are reading this book today. Grierson was working on his concept of democratic propaganda just before, and then during, WWII, which was the same time at which Hitler was utilizing the phrase. When we think critically about that fact, we realize that when we, readers, think about propaganda, we automatically think about the way in which it was used during WWII in Nazi Germany, because that is the context within which we typically learn about propaganda in. This context didn't exist for Grierson, because when he was thinking about propaganda, he was focused on using propaganda in a positive way to share the realities of the world through documentary film. Before Hitler, propaganda didn't have the grossly negative connotation that it does now, which means that as we read the word 'propaganda' in reference to Grierson, we have to check the connotation we see within the word and remember that the connotation behind the word when Grierson is utilizing it is very, very different.

With that understanding in mind, we now have to take a deep look at what Grierson believed to be 'democracy.' Because propaganda comes with such context, and a typically negative connotation, it's difficult to understand exactly how propaganda can be utilized in a beneficial way. Grierson saw democracy in a few ways, based on his education, but when it came down to it, he believed that "democracy is, above all, a *faith* - 'the faith that we the people [can], with hand and brain, run the world we [live] in,' and that *'a man is a man for a' that"* (Grierson, quoted in Babe, 2014, p. 97). Grierson really truly believed that if the people in the world were given the real and true facts, that they would be able to make the best decisions for themselves, their families, and their communities.

With that in mind, Grierson also understood what Robert Babe refers to as "the dogma of democracy" (Babe, 2014, p. 97). Babe notes that:

People simply *cannot* be experts on all matters of public concert. Nor are people necessarily the rational decision-makers the pure theory of democracy requires. Furthermore, the press cannot adequately inform people on public issues to the extent that the pure theory of democracy demands. [...] Grierson, therefore, set out to 'fill the gap in educational practices' as his way of retrieving authentic democracy (Babe, 2014, p. 97).

To Grierson, democracies "are political systems that encourage discussion, initiative, and activity at the local level" (Babe, 2014, p. 97). Grierson wanted to utilize the medium of documentary film to provide the people living at the local level with the information they required in order to understand the world around them. By doing so, Grierson believed he would be providing these people the opportunity to participate in an authentic democracy, because they were able to make decisions based on facts.

What was the basis of democratic propaganda, for Grierson? Education. Grierson felt that education was the right and only way to ensure that everyday folk could have enough of the facts to engage in the discussion, initiative, and activity that he believed made up the fundamental building blocks of democracy. Grierson's focus for his documentary films in Canada during the war was focused on building support for the war and finding ways to recruit up-and-coming Canadians to join the war effort. Though that is a topic for our next section, here, we will explore an example of print media and consider how it meets, differs from, and is opposite to Grierson's ideal of democratic propaganda.

Grierson had two fundamental beliefs about education that need to be understood before we look at our print example. First, Grierson believed that "if education is to be of value to workers and be supportive of democracy [...] it must become *less* rational, *less* analytical, *less* dispassionate, *more* emotive, *more* synoptic, and *more* persuasive: in sum, *more propagandistic*" (Babe, 2014, p. 99). Second, he believed that "education *for* democracy [...] requires that issues be simplified and presented in dramatic ways, first to attract attention, and second to stir people to action, initiative for him being 'the heart and soul of the democratic idea'" (Babe, 2014, p. 99). In this way, Grierson demonstrates his belief in story, because he feels that in order for education to be effective, it needs to tell a story. Stories, of course, help connect people to material, and by doing so, involves them in the story emotionally. Once people connect to a topic emotionally, the chances that they will remember the facts, share them with their friends, and even engage with the topic outside of their home, become higher.

Let's consider Grierson's two fundamental beliefs about education, as well as his thoughts on democratic propaganda, in relation to a popular type of print media: historical fiction. Exploring this concept, comparing and contrasting it with Grierson's beliefs, and considering whether or not it fits into the 'gatekeeping' box, will allow us to truly understand Grierson's thoughts and their practical applications. This understanding will lead us nicely into our discussion on Grierson and documentary film within the next chapter, when we'll explore the true focus of Grierson's democratic propaganda.

Historical fiction, in print, involves the writing of a story that's set sometime in history, often during a turning point in history. The story can include real or fictional characters, and can involve any amount of artistic license when it comes to the ways in which the characters interact and exist within their time period. Historical fiction's most criticized aspect is the realism, or lack thereof, within the story, since the time period in which the story is set is so key to the success and realism of the overall novel. Of course, there's more to historical fiction than just the time period:

> In some historical fiction, famous events appear from points of view not recorded in history, showing historical figures dealing with actual events while depicting them in a way that is not recorded in history. Other times, the historical event or time period complements a story's narrative, forming a framework and background for the characters' lives. Sometimes, historical fiction can be for the most part true, but the names of people and places have been in some way altered (Goodreads, 2021).

A great example of historical fiction in the Canadian realm is the children's series *Dear Canada*, which explores female protagonists within major historical events in world history. From a young Jewish girl living through the Holocaust in Germany to the Flu epidemic of 1918 to the Confederation in 1866, this series exists as the diary of young girls experiencing historical events firsthand. These books are written by famous Canadian female authors, and have won numerous awards, for the series and for individual books. Let's consider how these books would match up to Grierson's thoughts on democratic propaganda and education.

First, let's consider education. Are the *Dear Canada* books educational? Without a doubt. Not only does Scholastic, the publisher of the *Dear Canada* books, offer lesson plans for teachers that are utilizing the books in their classrooms, but the books also cover a wide breadth of history accurately, and in a way that children are able to understand. According to Trudy and Lynn Nelson, "historical narrative is more interesting and comprehensible to students than the expository writing of social studies textbooks" (1999, p 2-3). This fact lines up with Grierson's belief that education for democracy requires drama and story; in essence, a reason for the reader to stick around until the end of the book. By providing the *Dear Canada* books as a story, from the perspective of a child close in age to those who would be reading the book, the facts and stories that are shared within the book are made more real and believable to the series' young readers.

Do these books stir action in the young readers, though, as Grierson believes education should? Again, an argument can be made that yes, they do. Though the *Dear Canada* series is typically utilized for classroom learning, these books exist in nearly every Canadian library, and are popular books in general, which means that they are often read outside the classroom. Let's consider the book *Pieces of the Past*, which is a diary of a young girl who survived the Holocaust. Her diary details the story of her resettlement in Canada after the Holocaust, while sharing flashbacks to her Holocaust experience. In the end, she realizes that writing about her Holocaust experience helps her come to terms with the horrors she witnessed. How does this stir action in the young children reading these books? It gets them asking questions. As we all know, children are highly inquisitive, and one of their favourite questions is 'why.' When they begin applying that question to the Holocaust, they become more educated on one of the world's darkest moments in history.

Do the *Dear Canada* books exist as the 'democratic propaganda' that Grierson imagined? Yet again, the answer is yes. The books exist with a purpose: to educate children about major events in world history. There is strategy behind the ways in which they are presented; after all, they are presented in diary form, which permits a deep connection between the reader and the writer. "The diarist is a firsthand witness, retelling history and personalizing it in a way that no other form of literature can offer" (Gale, 2009), which demonstrates the power of the choice of form for these books. These books are provided with a specific lens, intent to share one specific story from a major historical event. Consider the fact that there are people in this world that believe that the Holocaust was a hoax; if we consider the fact that there are different opinions about how world events happened, it becomes fully clear that these books can be classified as 'democratic propaganda' because they spread information in a specific way, with a specific intention. The intention is not malicious in any way, which is where the 'democratic' aspect of the propaganda comes in. Instead, the focus is on sharing information with a specific audience with the intent that the audience will understand the information and take action on it in some way.

The question stands, then: does democratic propaganda constitute gatekeeping? In some ways, yes, it does. The key to democratic propaganda is not providing the real, unbiased facts; instead, democratic propaganda exists on the basis that the facts provided to an audience will be dramatized and persuasive to ensure that the audience will engage with them. This fact in itself distinguishes democratic propaganda as gatekeeping, because whomever is making the decision about which facts will be shared, how persuasive and dramatized they will be, and who the facts will be shared with, is making the decisions of a gatekeeper. Does this mean that the gatekeeping is sinister in nature? Not in all cases - in fact, it could be argued that in the case of the *Dear Canada* books, the gatekeeper has an important job of maintaining truth to the historical event while finding a way to replicate the events in a way that children can understand without being terrified of for the rest of their lives. In cases like these, it can be argued that gatekeeping is beneficial; though at the same time, the opposite can be argued, because who is to say that it isn't a parent's job to decide what material their child can and cannot handle when they are young?

Our exploration of John Grierson's communication thought will continue when we begin to discuss digital media, but exploring the basis of his thoughts on education and democratic propaganda have proved both fascinating and insightful as we move along our discussion of Canadian communication theory, Canadian media, and gatekeeping. Let's keep Grierson's communication thought in mind as we move through the remainder of the theorists we will consider in regards to print media, but don't forget - Grierson played a major part in Canadian documentary film, which we will explore in the next chapter.

Through the Lens: Gertrude Joch Robinson

The final theorist we will discuss in relation to print media is a notable female Canadian communication theorist: Gertrude Joch Robinson. Of course, in the spirit of saving the best until last, we have to understand that Robinson's work is primarily focused on gatekeeping and truth, which means that all the discussions we've had about other communication theories will culminate in this section as we explore her work. Before we explore her work, however, let's take a moment to get acquainted with her life, and why she is considered such an important Canadian communication theorist.

Gertrude Joch Robinson was born in Hamburg, Germany, between WWI and WWII, to a German father and an American mother. She lived through the beginnings of WWII during her youth; about her experience, she says ""I remember being bombed every night, terrified," Robinson says of the indelible memory of the Allies' carpet bombing. As a teenager, she learned a useful skill, or strategy, to deal with terror: "You just act as if life is normal"" (Robinson, quoted in Stiehm, 2014). After the war, her family moved to Swarthmore, in the United States, and Robinson enrolled in the local college, where she focused her studies on ethics and aesthetics. In 1950, Robinson joined the MA program at the University of Chicago, where she prepared her MA thesis: ""The Concept of Verification in Russell's and Dewey's Theory of Knowledge"" (Babe, 2014, p. 208).

Robinson's intellectual focus was put on hold during the 1950s, when she bore six children with her husband. After the sixth child, "she was diagnosed as tubercular and forced to convalesce for six months in a sanitarium at Urbana, Illinois (her husband having attained a teaching position at the University of Illinois in 1956)" (Babe, 2014, p. 209). After her time at the sanitarium, she went on to become a PhD student at the University of Illinois, and completed her doctoral dissertation in 1968. 1970, though, was when her connection to Canadian Communication theory began. "In 1970, she was hired by McGill's Sociology Department, where she began teaching a course on Canadian mass communication" (Babe, 2014, p. 210). Courses and studies on Canadian communication theory were slim at this time, and Robinson dove headfirst into the challenge, spending the next twenty years establishing and growing a communication program at McGill.

Of course, there is much more to Gertrude Joch Robinson's life than just what is mentioned above, but as with all the communication theorists we will discuss in this book, there simply isn't enough time or pages to dedicate to their entire life's story, which could fill books upon books. What we have provided you above is intended to be just enough to provide you with the context you require to understand why Robinson considers communication theory through the specific lens that she does. Before we dive into the communication theory that she introduced, though, we need to explore a theory that grounds much of Robinson's work: symbolic interactionism. By understanding the basics of symbolic interactionism, we will then be able to understand exactly how and why Robinson's work exists in the way that it does.

In their book *A First Look at Communication Theory*, Em Griffin and his colleagues define a symbolic interaction as: "the ongoing use of language and gestures in anticipation of how the other will react; a conversation" (2015, p. 54). In this way, a symbolic interaction is more than just a conversation: it's a conversation that's focused on using language and gestures that anticipate the way in which others in the conversation will react. Let's briefly explore the three core principles of symbolic interactionism: meaning, language, and thinking.

When Herbert Blumer, the theorist that coined the phrase 'symbolic interactionism' began his studies, he utilized "the premise that *humans act towards people or things on the basis of the meanings that they assign to those people or things*. Facts don't speak for themselves; it's our interpretation that counts. And once people define a situation as real, it's very real in its consequences" (Griffin et al, 2015, p. 55). For symbolic interactionists, meaning and interpretation are key: the way in which we understand the world around us is the way in which we construct our reality. Whether or not our meanings or interpretations are generally correct is, essentially, irrelevant: once we have defined a situation or idea as real, the concept itself is functionally real for us. This concept will tie in specifically to Gertrude Joch Robinson's thoughts on truth, and how it exists.

As noted by Griffin and his colleagues, "Blumer's second premise is that *meaning arises from the social interaction that people have with each other.* In other words, meaning is not inherent in an object; it's not pre-existent with a state of nature. Meaning is negotiated through the use of *language* - hence the term *symbolic interactionism*" (2015, p. 55). Readers, take a moment and look around you. Are the names of anything sitting near you logical in any way? Why is a book referred to as a book? Why do we refer to the action of expelling sound and breath loudly from one's mouth as screaming? Who decided that when we type, the buttons that we press are called keys, and those keys make up a keyboard? All of the words that we use are essentially arbitrary until they are given meaning. How are words given meaning? Through discourse, of course.

The third premise that Blumer worked on was "that an *individual's interpretation of symbols is modified by his or her own thought processes*" (Griffin et al, 2015, p. 57). Have you ever rehearsed a phone call or a conversation in your mind before it actually happened? Blumer would refer to that as minding, or "an inner dialogue used to test alternatives, rehearse actions, and anticipate reactions before responding; self talk" (Griffin et al, 2015, p. 57). This process involves us attempting to step into the shoes of the person that we will be conversing with in order to prepare for the conversation, and hopefully steer it in the way that we want. Perhaps we're trying to find good, scientific reasons to convince our parents we really do need that new xbox game. Maybe we're trying to convince our wife that we should spend a full day at the local waterpark, even though it's ridiculously expensive. Either way, we're taking the time to attempt to understand their perspectives and opinions so that we can be successful in our case.

There is far more to symbolic interactionism than what we've covered above, but we will dive more deeply into these concepts as we move into Gertrude Joch Robinson's work in communication theory. Because her theory has such a strong basis within symbolic interactionism, more of the theory will be interspersed within her work to help us further our understanding of her theories. That's not to say that her theory is symbolic interactionism, however: her theory takes its roots in symbolic interactionism, but grows into something unique and powerful on its own. How unique and powerful, you ask? Let us take a look. To begin, we'll explore her theory about the basis of truth: what is truth, and who is it the truth to?

Robinson takes a firm stance on truth, and what it constitutes. To her, "there are no 'raw data' - not even in the physical sciences. Interpretation, rather, is key. But interpretation is always couched in a social context" (Babe, 2014, p. 212). To her, then, truth doesn't exist in terms of scientific facts, because those facts can't exist without social context. Let's consider it this way. If the authors of this book were to do an experiment today, with the goal of testing the pH of a variety of liquids, we would do exactly that. Chances are, there would be a variety of pH's depending on the types of liquids we tested. Now, for the results to have meaning, the authors would need to have context for those results. For example, we would need to know what each pH means - whether it is acidic or basic - and have some understanding of what liquids we would expect to be acidic or basic, so we could place our findings within the context of other findings. Our raw data, or our findings, would mean very little without the ability to interpret them, and to interpret them, we would require the social context that includes other experiments, understanding of pH and the pH testing process, and more.

How does this concept or there being no 'raw data' translate outside of the scientific realm? Well, it comes down to the concept of truth. In Robinson's own words about truth, she said:

> I reject, in other words, a theory of 'truth' defined in terms of a one-to-one correspondence, because humans are 'symbol using animals; whose *understandings* [sic] of their social realities change not only themselves, but what those realities *mean*. Example: the [1999] nurses' strike in Montreal was initially interpreted as being about pay and working conditions. Now, seven days later, the nurses have turned the meaning of the strike into one about 'the safety of patients in a hospital system which has been badly mismanaged by the PQ government.' This government induced the scarcity of doctors and nurses through a buy-out and is perpetuating unsafe conditions by not paying nurses enough to attract new ones (Robinson, quoted in Babe, 2014, p. 213).

In this way, Robinson argues that truth is changeable, based on the social construction of our reality. To use her own example, it was true that the nurses strike began due to pay and working conditions, and it is also true that the strike evolved to become about the safety of patients within their mismanaged hospital system. The fact that the strike began as one thing and finished as another doesn't make it invalid; instead, it proves the social constructionist viewpoint that truth can be changed based on the social realities and the meaning of those social realities.

To use another example, let's consider a popular debate topic: whether pineapple belongs on pizza. Now, perhaps your starting stance is that pineapple doesn't belong on pizza. Your parents never put pineapple on pizza, so you learned that it didn't belong, you teased friends that put pineapple on pizza because it was weird of them - from your perspective - to put pineapple on pizza. Then, one day, you ended up trying a Hawaiian pizza, and actually really enjoying it. Now, at the beginning, the truth to you was that pineapple didn't belong on pizza. After trying pineapple on pizza and realizing that you enjoyed it, your social reality shifted, and your truth then became that pineapple can belong on pizza. Were you right or wrong in either stance? Not at all - there is no right answer as to whether or not pineapple belongs on pizza because the truth of the matter is individual, and depends on a person's preference.

Now, Robinson's focus on truth can be applied to much more than whether or not pineapple belongs on pizza. In fact, Robinson actually applied her theory on the basis of truth and the social construction of reality to consider gatekeeping within Canadian news media. Since the news media fits within the definition of print media, let's take a moment to explore Robinson's research on gatekeeping within Canadian news media, and then apply her theories to a modern example of gatekeeping within the media.

One example of gatekeeping within news media that Robinson explored was the difference in reporting from French-language and English-language newspapers as regards the October Crisis. Now, for those of you who don't recognize the October Crisis, let's take a moment and provide you with some background and context. The October Crisis took place in the fall of 1970 in Quebec, and "was the culmination of a long series of terrorist attacks perpetrated by the Front de Liberation du Quebec (FLQ), a militant Quebec independence movement between 1963 and 1970 (McIntosh & Cooper, 2020). Robert Babe also explains that the October Crisis "entailed the kidnapping and eventual release, fifty-nine days later, of British trade commissioner James Cross, by the [FLQ], and within that period also the kidnapping and murder of Quebec's Labour and Immigration minister, Pierre Laporte (Babe, 2014, p. 214). Of course, this event was heavily covered within news media, and Robinson compared the coverage by French news media and English news media to establish what the differences, if any, were within their coverage.

Robinson's focus on this specific event and the resulting coverage between two different types of news media was a result of her interest in social constructionism. She believed that "the crisis provided 'a unique opportunity for exploring in greater detail how English and French Canadians conceive of their alternate realities and what implications these conceptions have for their theories of communications and political behaviour'" (Robinson, quoted in Babe, 2014, p. 214). Of course, being able to read about and analyze the difference in language utilized to discuss the October Crisis is one thing, but establishing the truth that each news outlet saw within the October Crisis and how they were encouraging or not encouraging action on the part of their readers would lead Robinson to some fascinating discoveries.

It comes without reasonable surprise that Robinson did find some fairly big distinctions and differences in the way that the English and French news media reported on the October Crisis:

> Although the English and French dailies afforded approximately equal front-page space to stories focusing on 'kidnapping' and 'security,' the French dailies devoted significantly more attention to: 'negotiations,' 'religious aspects/funeral,' 'the position of the Federal Government,' 'the position of the Quebec government,' and 'time.' English papers, in contrast, emphasized 'manhunt,' 'the War Measures Act,' 'murder,' and 'Parliament' (Babe, 2014, p. 215).

Though the reporting was occurring on the same event, the focus of the articles differed between the English and the French: where the French news media were more focused on negotiation and rescue of captives, the English news media were more focused on hunting down those at fault for this event. By recognizing the difference between the two types of news media, Robinson was able to explore the ways in which news media played into the idea of truth and reality within a social constructionist viewpoint. "Robinson concluded that her findings affirmed the 'social construction of reality' thesis, which proposes that people learn about themselves and their world through a stock of symbols that are consistently selected and used by those living in the culture" (Babe, 2014, p. 215). By noting the use of specific words that focused either on retribution and punishment or negotiations and rescue, Robinson was able to study the ways in which the English and French communities viewed the October crisis, and how their viewpoints differed based on the reporting by their respective news media.

Now, the question remains: was Robinson technically studying gatekeeping in the above example? The authors of this book would argue yes, because the way in which the news media were framing the October Crisis had a direct impact on the way in which their respective readers understood and viewed the Crisis. If, for example, one reader only read one magazine, and didn't receive information from other sources about the October Crisis, that reader would likely adopt the viewpoint of the news medium from which he was reading, simply because it was the only source of information he had. If the focus of that medium was on the capture and punishment of the perpetrators, that would be his focus - not intentionally because that was the aspect of the story he focused on, but because that is the focus of the news media. On the other hand, if the same reader had taken the time to gather sources from many news media outlets, he would have had a better opportunity to decide which 'truth' he wanted to put his faith in and believe in, and therefore adopt it into his social reality.

If we filter the essence of Robinson's study, we can apply it to a variety of gatekeeping examples. At its most basic, Robinson's theory argues that truth, and the concept of truth, is a social construct, and is dependent on the world around us. Because of this fact, things that are true to the authors of this book might not be true to some of you - our readers. That would mean that if we were in a position of power and able to make gatekeeping decisions on certain topics, we might choose differently about whether certain information would be shared, and if so, what lens it would be shared with. This fact is something we need to consider as we take in information around us, because it reminds us that we need to be thinking about where the information came from, what lens it comes through, and whether or not there might be additional information that was quashed at the source.

Gertrude Joch Robinson was an incredible, trailblazing, female Canadian communication theorist. Her theories speak directly to gatekeeping and truth, and are still poignant and true to this day. When we think about gatekeeping, particularly within Canada, we have to think of Robinson, because without her theories, we would be more willing to accept the information provided to us because we wouldn't have the theory and studies to back up the fact that everyone views the world differently, and depending on our positions of power, we have the ability to keep certain gates of our own. Her theories serve as a reminder for us to consider our positions and how we share or don't share information - if we find ourselves in a gatekeeping position, we should always return to Robinson's theories and wonder how and why we are serving the best interest of the community, and what assumptions we are making about truth and best interests in general.

Conclusion

Canadian communication theorists and theories that study gatekeeping are relatively widespread throughout the field of communication theory. Though we only touched on the theories of four Canadian communication theorists in this book, and how those theories related specifically to gatekeeping and Canadian media, we learned how to apply those theories in our everyday lives. Now, when we pick up a book in a bookstore or a magazine from a newsstand, we have the tools to carefully and critically consider all the factors that brought that piece of print media into our hands, and we are able to analyze the truth and propaganda that may be included inside.

Print media is found all around us: from books to texts to pdf documents, the written word is a particularly important part of our world. It's time for us now to switch gears and dive into what might be considered a more popular type of media these days. As we do so, we can continue to apply the theories of Harold Adams Innis, Marshall McLuhan, John Grierson, and Gertrude Joch Robinson to the media we are about to discuss, and take a much wider and more considered look at a particularly interesting and reasonably new form of media: digital media. As we do so, we will further our understanding and knowledge of gatekeeping, Canadian media, and Canadian communication theory.

Chapter 3:
Digital Media

Canada has an interesting relationship with the idea of gatekeeping, as you have learned so far. However, Canada's gatekeeping effects don't begin and end with print media. Digital and analogue media are also subject to the ideas and practices of gatekeeping. Canadian digital media holds a particularly interesting connection with gatekeeping in this medium due to the landscape of digital media, how it airs across the country, and the rules that it employs. In this section we will explore some of the different forms that make up the all encompassing term of digital media, as well as how gatekeeping theory lives within the boundaries of those forms. Now, let's explore what constitutes digital media.

What is Digital Media?

Digital or analogue media is a term that we will use in this text to encompass any type of audio or visual-based media that is transmitted digitally. This includes film, television, radio, and even the podcasts you may be listening to right now. Of course, these types of media can branch out into their own genres, each that may employ gatekeeping theory in their own way. For example, television can include the hottest new drama show that has caught everyone's attention and the news channels that provide Canadians across the country with information they need to know on a daily basis. As you can see, one form of digital media can impact its audiences in vastly different ways, not to mention the fact that sections of the audience may experience the forms differently from other sections. In this sense, these forms of genres within digital media can become complex and difficult to parse. For this reason, we will observe these forms from a more general viewpoint, occasionally reaching into the minute intricacies of each medium to further explain their relationship to gatekeeping.

As far as Canada's relationship with digital media goes, there is one large part of the media landscape that sets Canada apart from many other countries - the Canadian Broadcasting Corporation (CBC). The CBC has been a part of Canada's media outlook since the early 1900s, and has since gone on to become a part of the identity of many Canadian citizens. There are other privately owned production companies that occupy the digital media realm in Canada as well. Some of the larger entities include Bell, Corus, Rogers, and Quebecor. While much smaller than their American counterparts, these entities hold a great amount of influence in Canada on what the public hears through the digital media that they consume. Most of these companies are focused on the realms of television and radio.

Canada's film industry is much smaller than that of the United States, as most large films produced or made in Canada often have a larger American production company at least co-producing it or heavily funding it. One of Canada's largest film production companies is another publicly owned organization called the National Film Board of Canada, or the NFB, which was founded by documentarian John Grierson. Let's jump in and explore some of these types of digital media. We'll start with documentary film, including the NFB, and how John Grierson's idea of gatekeeping relates to modern Canadian media.

Documentary Film

When we think of a documentary, whether it takes the form of a film, television show, or radio program, we don't necessarily think of that specific media's link to gatekeeping right away. The definition of documentary according to the Cambridge Dictionary is "a film or television or radio program that gives facts and information about a subject" (Cambridge Dictionary, n.d.). By definition, then, a documentary should be a program that gives all of the necessary facts and information about the subject it focuses on. While this is a novel idea, there will almost always be some form of gatekeeping in a documentary. Sometimes it may be harmless, leaving facts out that aren't necessary for the audience's focus of that story, but other times it may appear more malicious to some as an attempt to ensure that information given in a documentary supports the subject the creator is focusing on while omitting information that may be pertinent to the discussion.

When speaking about the relationship between gatekeeping and documentary films within the borders of Canada, it is difficult to avoid discussing John Grierson. We discussed Grierson earlier, and his ideas around gatekeeping and propaganda, but it would be remiss to not observe his innovations within this section as well. As an integral part of the creation of the National Film Board, Grierson holds a specifically interesting outlook on Canada's unique situation in the public funding of our media. However, we must speak of Grierson when speaking about documentaries because he was incredibly fundamental in the creation of documentary filmmaking.

Though Grierson spent much of his career helping produce films rather than actually create them, he did venture into the role of filmmaker a small number of times. In these films we can clearly see Grierson's idea of teaching through propaganda in his films. Grierson's first documentary feature, *Drifters*, focused on the Scottish herring fisheries. In line with Grierson's ideas, he took on the roles of writer, director, and editor (Babe, p. 90). This auteur approach to his documentaries also makes for interesting techniques to be used. For one, the film shows that Grierson's creative mind was not limited when tackling real world issues, as he was focused on telling the story he intended to tell rather than the reality of some situations. As it is a silent film, it was in Grierson's hands how he wanted to portray the workers through the intertiles as the workers could not express themselves through their own speech. Grierson was also to construct scenes in a way that would allow him to speak to specific ideas as he was the editor. One of the main ideas conveyed in the film is that of modernism. *Drifters* was also incredibly important because it was an essential piece that allowed his documentary film movement to launch into the wider world.

When thinking of Grierson's thoughts on propaganda, those which may even be seen as totalitarian, it makes sense that his chosen medium of expression was that of documentary filmmaking. This is because in the role of a director in filmmaking, at least in film where the filmmaker is attempting to communicate their ideas or the ideas of others, it is important that they have total control of the process. If they do not have control of that process, it is much more likely that the film will fail to convey the ideas or emotions that the filmmaker was originally intending. Documentaries can be created on a fairly low budget and without a large crew, which can give the filmmaker more control to shape the intended message to the viewer.

Another example of Grierson's use of gatekeeping comes from his time as commissioner of the National Film Board. During the second world war, the propaganda films put out by the NFB did not appear as others of its kind from across the world did. The NFB propaganda films ``contained little or no hatemongering [sic] or violence" (Babe, p. 93). This was a conscious decision made by Grierson because he knew once the war had concluded, the world would need to work together again and he wanted to help the world make that peaceful transition. In altering the propaganda films to speak to certain messages that he wanted to communicate and teach his audience with, Grierson was gatekeeping the information that he portrayed to the audience. This demonstrates Grierson's idea of being a "totalitarian for good" (Babe, 2014, p. 95), in that information can be molded in order to encourage discussion, initiative, and activity at local levels and within communities, which was also his primary idea of what a democracy should look like.

One aspect that also comes into play when speaking of documentaries and gatekeeping is that of financing. One's holistic vision for a creative project can be watered down or even dismissed based on the demands of those financing the project. Financing also adds a whole new layer to the gatekeeping, as the fianancers likely have their own ideas or messages they want to communicate with the audience, separate from the creators. Though this is an issue that plagues many forms of media, it is still very prevalent. It does not matter if the funding comes from a public source, like much of the NFB's funding did, or a private entity, the fianancer of a product is the one with the final say and therefore will have their own ideas that might find their way into the film.

The idea of gatekeeping information in order to speak to the ideas that you want to is something that is very ingrained into documentary features. While documentaries are still today considered to be a look at some kind of truth or fact, the real truth or fact of the matter is that documentaries are still a creative expression. Those expressions, while based within a reality that some people in the world live within, are still crafted in order to tell a story in order to convey the thoughts and ideas of it's creator. From journalistic documentaries to more creative artistic outputs, documentaries will always have some form of gatekeeping that can be found within.

In Grierson's ideas of documentaries and filmmaking in general, there is space to find the idea of auteur theory. According to the Encyclopaedia Britannica, auteur theory "holds that the director, who oversees all audio and visual elements of the motion picture, is more to be considered the 'author' of the movie than is the writer of the screenplay" (n.d.). This may relate to Grierson's firm belief of what the purpose of his documentaries were: an educational tool that used storytelling methods to further engage his audience into learning the information he was feeding them. While the idea of an auteur is much more aligned with theatrical films, a director for documentary may be even more so an auteur than those who work on a fictional or semi-fictional film. This is because documentaries often have much smaller teams, and most likely do not have a script; instead, the creators vision comes through the experiences caught on camera, and how those sequences are edited together.

While some documentarians have different ideas of how to frame their stories, or even how much of themselves they should include in them, it can be argued that they always use some form of gatekeeping, to varying degrees. Some may choose to narrate the viewer's journey, explain the information that the viewers are seeing on screen, or even appear in the film. Others may choose to stay out of the film as much as they can, only making themselves responsible for capturing images and piecing them together into something engaging for their audience. Both may actually gatekeep information in separate, but similar ways. The first kind of creator may describe a scene in a way that could misrepresent what the subject or environment was actually experiencing. With those who only keep their influence behind the camera, documentarians may pick and choose scenes or place scenes in such a way that might omit information in order to make the audience feel or think in a specific way. Neither of these options is inherently good or evil, but rather can be used for either - just as Grierson had posited. However, studios and production companies can come between the creator and their vision, as stated previously. They may provide their own ideas on the piece of media, in so far as performing their own gatekeeping through shaping the narrative or theme of the documentary.

Documentaries are likely to have some form of gatekeeping, regardless of and even because of what the creator is trying to convey to their audience through their film. However, it is up to the documentarians themselves to give an honest representation or interpretation of their subject that must take into account how their representation of that subject can sway and influence those who view their documentary. Part of this process is gaining the respect and trust of their subject, and just as with anything in life, if one is to break that trust a bond is broken, so it is imperative for a creator to not lose the trust of their subject or their audience. We will explore more of this aspect in a future section of the book, but for now let's move into similar territory to that of documentary film: film and television.

Film and Television

Before we get into the idea of gatekeeping in film, let us first consider Canada's film industry quickly. While Canada has a great reputation when it comes to television broadcasting, its film industry is not as well known, maybe even under-appreciated. In terms of Canadian films, there aren't really any large private production or distribution companies. Canada's film industry, while slowly growing, is incredibly small in comparison to its southern neighbours in Hollywood. In fact, most Canadian-produced films receive much of their funding from the Canadian government through various forms of funding and incentives. In the 2017/2018 year, at least 59% of the financing provided to Canadian theatrical feature film releases were from public sources, whether that be directly from the Federal and Provincial Governments or from a program created by the Canadian Government to provide funding to Canadian films (Canadian Media Producers Association, p.53).

What Canada does have that some countries do not is a publicly-owned broadcaster - the Canadian Broadcasting Corporation, or CBC. Just as is the case with many of the forms of digital media in Canada, the Canadian Government is a major media producer. The CBC was created in 1936 by the Canadian Parliament in order to subdue the growing influence of American radio on the Canadian airwaves (CBC Radio Website, n.d.). While the CBC continued to regain control over the radio, the CBC wouldn't move into the television landscape until nearly twenty years later, in 1952 (CBC Archive, n.d.). The CBC's creation and its further development were all done to promote primarily Canadian content over the media broadcast throughout the country, in one way or another. This action by the Canadian Government displays gatekeeping theory in that it was an action taken with the purpose of the country and government having more control in the information delivered to its national audience. While national broadcasters as gatekeepers have their fans as well as their detractors, there is no doubt that the CBC has played a vital role in Canadian media for the past 85 years.

Another publicly created organization that provides a strong backbone to Canadian produced films is the National Film Board, which we spoke about when discussing John Grierson and documentary films. Being created shortly after the CBC, the NFB purpose according to Grierson was to "be the 'eyes of Canada'" (Government of Canada, 2021). Over the years the mandate for the NFB has changed, including in 1950 when the mandate set was "to produce and distribute and to promote the production and distribution of films designed to interpret Canada to Canadians and to other nations" (Government of Canada, 2021). While the NFB's strategic reports today are much more structured with many values and actions, it is interesting to look at the early years of the NFB through a gatekeeping lens. Much like the CBC, it appears this may have been a part of the Canadian government to gain back more control over their airwaves from the American media companies that were slowly impeding into their territory. By promoting Canadian culture and values to those across the country, they were hoping to send consistent messaging to its citizens, rather than from a mishmash of Canadian and American media sources. They would be able to give Canadians the information they wanted to receive, or that promoted culture, and keep that influence out of Americans hands.

While you may not think of fictional TV and film in terms of gatekeeping theory, the fact is that every television show or movie uses techniques that could be considered gatekeeping. That is because these visual mediums employ certain techniques to help their audiences suspend their disbelief as to fully immerse themselves in the piece of media. These techniques often go on behind the scenes, and are not presented to the viewer.: the viewer might only notice the techniques and camera tricks if they have some knowledge of filmmaking and are keeping an eye out for said tricks as they watch.

The gatekeeping doesn't just end with the production of a film, however. In fact, gatekeeping can be employed before and after the filming has been completed. There is a certain level of gatekeeping that takes place in both the pre-production and approval process, as well as in a film or television series distribution. Many prospective writers and filmmakers tend to point out how the industry employs gatekeeping methods, which are in place primarily because of the high risk that comes with investing in a film. In order to ensure that they see a return on their investment, prospective producers and financiers will often be much more favourable in offering funds to an established creator who has a decent track record, with new creators fighting an uphill battle to get their creation funded and distributed to a larger audience due to their lack of a reputable past as far as financial success goes (Wandering, 2015).

Whether you find yourself in the movie theatre with a bag of popcorn waiting to see the next summer blockbuster, or at home watching the daily news broadcast, you are more than likely to find yourself subjected to some form of gatekeeping. That is because the advertisements shown before, during, and after the piece of media has played are likely subject to gatekeeping theory. Gatekeeping has a place in the advertisements shown to those consuming a piece of visual, digital media through those behind the scenes in a couple of different ways. The first is decided by who has paid enough money to have their product shown. This is a huge reason why most of the adverts you will see on popular television programs are for products that are already hugely popular and have the buying power to put themselves in those positions. The second is decided by the viewer themselves through the broadcaster choosing adverts that are pertinent or front of mind for the audiences viewing the programs (Davie, n.d.). For example, you are less likely to see an advert for swimwear in the middle of a cold Canadian winter than you would be during the summer season.

Another aspect that can be considered for gatekeeping is the director or the creator of a film. We spoke of auteur theory in the documentary film section, and it absolutely applies for fictional or semi-fictional digital media. While the director of one of these types of films or television programs may not hold the same control as a documentarian does, in some respects because of the amount of funding or the type of funding they may receive, the director or creator of a film or television program may actually have more control. If they are trusted by the film financiers and producers as was mentioned above, they can be given the opportunity to create a story exactly how they see it; within or outside of the rules of reality. From the inception to the idea to how that idea is filmed, recorded, edited and so on, the director or creator can have the control to withhold whatever they may like from it's audience until the moment it would create a larger impact to the viewer. However, this is very rarely the case when it comes to television and film creators. Again, because of the trust and convincing that is needed to make their ideas come true, they may never see the idea in their head fully actualized due to budget constraints or differences of thinking with those financing the piece of media.

This can be a problem for privately funded pictures which may seem obvious, but it can be an issue with public funding as well, though in those cases it would most likely happen before a film can get off the ground. That is because an organization like the NFB may have their own strategic plans that are implemented to lay out what the purpose of the organization is and what their goals are for a certain period of time. Let's take the early iteration of the NFB for example, in 1950 where they wanted to produce films to "interpret Canada to Canadians and to other nations" (Government of Canada, 2021). During this period of their existence, they would be looking to produce films that displayed some idea of Canada and of Canadian-ness; because of this, they may have not produced films that were focused on something a committee did not believe was "Canadian" enough.

This form of gatekeeping is not necessarily a bad or a good thing - it is just the fact of reality. In one sense it is a fact of reality that receiving funding for an idea is extremely difficult and it may call into question if auteur theory can really exist. Creating a piece of film or televised media is incredibly complicated and creative, often requiring collaboration in order to get an idea produced into something more. With more collaborators placed into the equation, do they have a hand in gatekeeping as well? Indeed, everyone from the cinematographer or camera operators to the gaffer and their lighting crew to the fianancers have a hand in gatekeeping information or the tricks of the trade from the viewer of the film or television program. It is through this gatekeeping of information that they are able to create the magic of film and television.

Radio

When it comes down to it, the gatekeeping that takes place over radio waves often comes from the producer or program director of a station, who is influenced by the organization that employs them. Whether it is a radio program, or the music that is being played, a certain level of gatekeeping exists in order to appeal to their target audience. Programmers may make their decision on what to play based upon record sales and tip sheets, and often there is pressure from record companies trying to get music by their artists played (Burns, 1997). Because the radio stations need to make money, they focus on the hit songs that trickle down from large record labels and are popular across the nation. This also leads to the local music scene having a more difficult time getting their music to a larger audience, as a radio programmer may choose to play more popular songs rather than give a smaller artist a chance, because they "want to play hits, not find them" (Burns, 1997). It's interesting that the programmers are actually the second level of gatekeeping that may hold artists from the public, as those artists that record companies put their investments into are the ones who will get pushed. Those who record labels condemn as not being capable of producing money-making songs have been given a harder experience of getting their music out to the public in the past.

However, and in some cases thankfully, this is not so much the case these days. With the birth of the internet and websites such as Bandcamp, which allows independent artists to share and sell their music with a wider audience, artists not backed by a record company today have an easier time getting their music to a wider audience. Musical streaming websites such as Spotify also give independent artists a fighting shot in sharing their audience with a wider, global audience. While musicians may still have an uphill battle when it comes to the giant money machines that make up the record industry, it has to be said that artists no longer need to rely on these companies to pick them up in order to gain fans and be successful.

One of the more important and interesting aspects of Canada's radio history wasn't even something that came out of Canada; rather, it was the encroaching grasp of the larger and much more prominent radio industry that came from the south. By the 1930s, the American radio industry had expanded its influence across the northern borders to the point that Canada decided to push back against the American influence. This is something we mentioned before in our sections on documentaries as well as television and film; however, it was radio that was the government's first target in expanding its influence across the country. Due to this influence, as well as religious institutions using radio to attack one another, the Canadian government stepped in and created the Royal Commission on Radio Broadcasting, also known as the Aird Commission in 1928. One year later the commission would provide a report to the Canadian government that "emphasized the importance of Canadian content on Canadian radio, while also envisioning radio as a potential agent for national unity" (McGowan, 2012).

In order to accomplish this, the Aird commission recommended that the government create a nationally owned broadcasting corporation in 1929, akin to the BBC in England (McGowan, 2012). This would lead to the creation of the Canadian Radio Broadcasting Commission or the CRBC in 1932. By 1936 the CRBC would be replaced with the recently born CBC or Radio-Canada (CBC Radio Website, n.d.).

This event is interesting to observe when looking through the lens of gatekeeping. The worry of the American radio industry overtaking any Canadian content over the airwaves was inspired at least partly by the idea of a loss of control. The American station, in the minds of those in the Aird commission, would fill Canadians minds with American content and start to strip away the Canadian identity. What this airwave invasion might also do is greatly reduce the Canadian governments influence on what would be broadcasted in the country. Because of this idea, a publicly-owned radio station was formed, so it would be easier to control the flow of information to the Canadian public, while also promoting Canadian values.

The Canadian Government may be one example of how gatekeeping is present with the world of Canadian radio. But let's look back at the radio stations and their programmers. How can gatekeeping exist on this level, specifically in the Canadian landscape? First off, the music industry in Canada definitely has influence as to choosing who they believe can make hits and pushing those artists. However, because of content rules and the goals of CBC radio, there are many smaller and independent record labels that may not have the capital of large record labels but need to take the chance on smaller Canadian artists and push their music. One of the reasons for this is that radio is actually subject to Canadian content requirements by the Canadian Government. Any privately owned radio station playing popular music must ensure that 35% of it is Canadian content. However, any CBC radio station must ensure that 50% of its popular music selections are Canadian content (Canadian Radio-television and Telecommunications Commission, 2002). These rules allow Canadian content to not be pushed out by the colossal amount of music that is produced by the incredibly wealthy music industries around the world, particularly from America. By doing this, the Canadian government is putting up a gate that allows Canadian content to leak through to the Canadian audiences around the country while limiting the influence of American content.

The other difference that is unique to Canada, at least when speaking comparatively to the United States, is our public broadcaster: CBC. The CBC has its own plan to achieve the organization's goals. For instance, their 2019 to 2022 strategic plan notes that one of their main goals is to be

"A Champion of Canadian Culture," with some of their subgoals including being "a champion for Canadian voices and stories in a world where the proliferation of foreign content could all to easily drown these out," and offering "solutions to the rising dominance of digital global players" (CBC/Radio-Canada, 2019). In holding these standards of promoting Canadian content, they are hoping to provide a form of barrier to foreign content, acting as a gatekeeper for the foreign content that they do allow through. They are also a form of gatekeeper with Canadian content, in the way that they can choose what Canadian content finds its way onto their radio programs. That is where the individual program directors for the radio stations that we discussed earlier on come into play: they ultimately get to pick and choose which Canadian content makes its way into a program.

The radio, while maybe not the most popular form of media anymore, definitely has its purpose in sharing Canadian music and content from coast-to-coast. In ensuring that they promote Canadian content, radio stations must also gatekeep both foreign and Canadian content in order to play music or other audio forms that at least a segment of the Canadian public is interested in listening to. In the end, the Canadian governments and CBC's goals to promote Canadian content in the midst of a constant flow of foreign content trying to flow into the country is admirable for Canadian artists who may not have the opportunity if some of the aforementioned actions had not taken place to include them. As long as Canadians continue to listen to the radio, they can count on their radio stations to play Canadian produced music.

Conclusion

In observing what the digital media landscape in Canada looks like and how it may use gatekeeping, we can see the ideas of two communication theorists on the subject at play, in particular. First are the ideas of democratic propaganda posited by John Grierson. As the Canadian Government holds a large amount of control over digital media in Canada through publicly funded organizations such as the CBC and NFB, they can help shape the landscape of what the digital media and digital content means and represents to Canadians from coast to coast. While the early iterations of these organization had a large focus on the idea of propaganda for good, the remnants of Grierson's influence and thoughts can be seen in the goals of both the NFB and CBC in providing Canadians with Canadian content, and by choosing to represent Canadian-ness in the media they produce and distribute.

Secondly comes the importance of Canadian culture within the wider media communications, proposed by Harold Adam Innis. As we learned, Innis believed that Canadian communication history was very much influenced by resource economics such as the fish and fur coat industries as the country was beginning to grow further west. With these industries growing, communication must follow and the messages of whatever digital media follows that trail follows. In this same line of thought, Innis also became increasingly worried about America's commercialism and the influence it may have on Canadian media and communications (Babe, 2014, p. 55). This thinking was obviously adopted by the Canadian Government in their creation of publicly funded media organizations in order to halt that growing influence of south to north, and keep the influence as Canadian as possible. This form of gatekeeping in order to prevent a greater American influence to engulf Canadian media shares the ideas of Innis' final worries and attempts to keep Canadian-ness a key part of the Canadian digital media identity.

In general, our discussion on gatekeeping and digital media has reminded us that the content we receive has been passed through a series of gates and gatekeepers before reaching our hands. When we consider digital media in terms of the communication theorists we discussed in chapter two, we realize that the content we receive digitally has been carefully curated not only to meet the government regulations surrounding that form of media, but also that the content may have been very different when the idea was originally proposed. Like we discussed in the second chapter, we have to carefully consider what content we are, and aren't, being provided, and why that might be. This conversation leads us to the final chapter of our book, where we will discuss a big question in terms of gatekeeping: how do gatekeeping and ethics collide?

Chapter 4:
The Ethics
of
Gatekeeping

Gatekeeping plays a key role in our exchange of information, as we can clearly see. In many cases, it can be fairly harmless, and sometimes can be used to good effect in streamlining information to best communicate with specific audiences. However, gatekeeping can also be used in malicious ways that are meant to cause harm, or in ways that help spread misinformation. This is why it is important that the act of gatekeeping be looked at through an ethical lens; that is, to bring into question the morality of gatekeeping. Before we get too far into the ethical stance of gatekeeping, let's take a deeper look at what ethics exactly are.

According to the Cambridge Dictionary, the primary definition of the word ethics is: "a system of accepted beliefs that control behaviour, especially such a system based on morals" (Cambridge Dictionary, n.d.). While philosophers struggle with the concepts of what makes good and evil, as well as what is the moral right in any given situation, groups of people might take those written thoughts and create their own sense of morality based around the structures that encapsulated their own lives. Our ideas of right and wrong - our notion of ethics - can come from many different places. In our personal lives, our ethics usually stem from aspects of our own lived history. One large aspect of how we set our worldview is in our childhood, and in the ways we were raised. Depending on how our parents or caregivers taught us lessons, and how those around us responded to our actions, we are set with a clear guideline of what behaviours are accepted by those around us. This continues through our teenage years, where our ethical conundrums are less about what actions will reap praise or admonishment, but rather of social norms and how actions are seen by those in society (Media Smart, n.d.). While our experiences in our formative years have a great impact on how we develop our own sense of morals, there are also larger institutions that shape one's ethical makeup outside of one's own internal intuitions. One of the largest examples would be the many religions that exist throughout our world, of which many have their own ideas of morality and ethics that those who practice and worship a particular religion must abide by. The question of morality can be asked of all of gatekeeping theory, not just gatekeeping that is used for ill-intent, and the ethics that we follow in regards to gatekeeping are built throughout our lives.

Other large organizations can develop their own ethics as well. Fields of study and occupations often develop their own ethical and moral codes in order to avoid taking advantage of those who may hold less power in a given situation. In scientific and social scientific fields for instance, an ethical code is often adhered to when committing to researching certain topics. The medical field in particular often has many interesting questions regarding the ethics of their services and interactions between a patient and the health official attending to them. Another interesting point in observing the medical field from an ethical and gatekeeping lens is that both seem to have their place in the field of study and the industry. There are studies that look into this aspect, such as the 2018 study *Narratives and Gatekeeping: making sense of triage nurses' practice* from Lars E.F. Johannessen, in which Lars explores the gatekeeping that exists for emergency service nurses in their decision making when it comes to deciding who is a so-called "trivial patient" and which patients need assistance right away. With this comes an ethical issue, in that they often, based on the information the patient gives them as well as their own knowledge, may give less credence to a patient that appears to have insignificant issues, at least compared to someone with more severe injuries. Similar situations can happen in our news media, whether it be journalists prioritizing news that will have a greater impact on their audience or documentarians not using a specific subject in their film because it does not fit in with the idea or story they are trying to tell. When exploring how the news media employs gatekeeping theory, ethics surely must follow. This is because when one uses gatekeeping to withhold a piece of information or an idea, the ethical question of how does this act impact another human being needs to be asked.

While those who work in the news media don't necessarily have the overwhelming heaviness that are often life and death situations that a nurse in triage may face, they have their own ethical dilemmas in how they operate and express a point -- whether fictional or literal -- to the general public. Let's take a moment to explore ethics and news media, whether it be writers, journalists, publishers or directors. Who creates the ethical systems and moral laws that they are supposed to follow? Well, actually, they do. The creators of news media have created their own codified ethical format to follow to ensure that they can easily understand who is doing things the "right way" and push those who don't follow these rules out of their circles (Singer, 2008, p. 63). In Canada, journalist practices are upheld to a standard of the ethical guidelines created by the Canadian Association of Journalists. By employing these guidelines, journalists are able to understand the moral boundaries of their work and where the line needs to be drawn when communicating with the general public.

While we are speaking about ethics in news media, and specifically about the role that journalists play as gatekeepers, an important component of their role to note is the concept of objectivity; that is, ensuring that the information that they are giving to their audience is absolutely true, no matter anyone's background or thoughts on the subject. The idea of objectivity may make sense in some fields, such as that of scientific research. Scientific truths are discovered and observed independently of an individual perception. However, subjectivity can still draw into the discussion and theories of these scientific events that are observed in order to explain what causes it. Journalism and the world of news media has an even more difficult relationship with objectivity. A journalist's most difficult task is then the act of removing themselves and their own thoughts from a story. When the journalist is able to act as a sole gatekeeper, this act of taking an objective stance may be easier for them. This is because they may be acting as an isolated party, removed from the world as the gatekeeper of information removed from emotions and opinions (Singer, 2008, p. 74-75). With this form of information exchange, the audience should be able to form their own opinions on the news based upon their own learnings and personal experiences. However, journalists and others that create news media no longer hold the all powerful role as gatekeeper, if that was a role they ever truly held in the first place.

In terms of our news, journalists were the primary gatekeepers for many years. While journalists today still hold some amount of power through their extension of information, they are a much smaller part of today's exchange of news. With the rise of social media and the internet, each person may commit to some form of gatekeeping in their day-to-day exchange of information with others through these media. When journalists and news organizations were the primary gatekeepers in the news world, the questions of ethics, it's important to remember that: "while some will be tipping the moral scales one way or another, [they] were at least slightly more structured and codified due to the rules put in place by those who taught journalism, journalism professionals and the news institutions that employed journalists" (Singer, 2008). Now, the ethical outlook of journalism is much less structured and more open to each individual's own interpretations on how their actions may affect others. With social media only a few clicks away for most people, journalists or not, everyone who posts on a social media platform could be subject to some form of ethical criticism. Nevertheless, journalists working in both print and digital news media must continue to uphold the standards of their profession through the guidelines they have given themselves, and recognize where gatekeeping information may be ethically wrong.

The ethical component of gatekeeping can also be explored within the confines of film and documentary films. The NFB has their own code of values and ethics, much like any other organization. Because the NFB is a publicly funded organization, it is imperative for them to abide by their code of ethics in order to achieve the trust of the public's view of the NFB and other public sector organizations. However, this code of ethics is only assigned to the organization's employees, not the creators who are funded and distributed by the NFB. This is an interesting point to make, because the NFB has to be careful when deciding which projects they can attach their name to, because the documentarian and filmmaker has to set their own rules and tell the stories and ideas they want to explore.

Documentarians then must set their own rules, maintain their conscientiously established boundaries, and avoid crossing lines set by both themselves and their subjects. Though they also must acknowledge that there may always be an audience member who questions whether or not something should have been filmed and deems it unethical (Cipriani, 2014).

In this sense, looking at the gatekeeping within film, particularly documentary film, is most interesting due to its creative structure. In film, gatekeeping can be used to create a narrative that the creator of the film wants the audience to learn about or achieve a certain sense of emotion from. Is doing this ethical? That depends on the filmmaker's own ethical code and how that fits into their artistic vision for a project.

Many people believe that documentaries are too informational, though there are certainly many documentaries that are focused on achieving an audience's emotional reaction. It is important to note, at this point, that the documentary film is still a form of expressive art (Nichols, 2006). A documentarian isn't held by the same guidelines that a journalist is, like we pointed out earlier.

For fictional or semi-fictional works, either distributed through print or by digital means, the ethics in terms of gatekeeping can be called into question in regards to the creation of the text or how the piece of media is produced. Regarding the first point, the creation of such a text may be based on someone or something that existed, but the facts of the story may become stretched out in order to fit something exciting or engaging into the narrative. In this situation, information that may be pertinent to the real life event may be withheld or eliminated in order to tell the story that the creator wants to tell. This could cause an ethical dilemma in that it may hurt or damage those that were closely engaged with the real event or person. Regarding the second point, a studio or publisher may deploy gatekeeping in order to give those who have more experience or success the upper hand in giving out funding or signing contracts with. These types of decisions are business motivated, of course, as studios or publishers are just choosing the safest options that they know will make them money. The ethics of this kind of gatekeeping are much less clear in many situations. If a studio or a publisher is going out of their way to not take someone's work seriously, that could be ethically wrong. However, sometimes there are just so many ideas that get sent to these gatekeepers that there will inevitably be some they don't find value in, or that do not fit into their organizational goals. Because there is not really an ethical code for gatekeeping what stories will be produced over others, this can be a much more grey area of ethics.

As we have discussed, gatekeeping exists within every piece of media in some facet of its creation or distribution. Canadian media, news media included, must hold some form of ethical code or policies that promote ethical behaviours. Within these organizational, occupational, or even individual ethical codes, it is important that the idea of gatekeeping is captured and carefully considered. When gatekeeping is removed from ethical discussions, the results can be disastrous; for example, if a group or individual is hurt or their reputation is damaged due to the information that a gatekeeper withheld. It's important to remember as well that it has been argued that gatekeeping can also be used for good, much like John Grierson proclaimed with his ideas on documentary film and democratic propaganda. It would take books upon books to fully explore the impacts of ethics on gatekeeping; after all, as we discovered, there isn't always a clear line that defines what is and isn't ethical when it comes to gatekeeping. What we have established, though, is a brief introduction to ethics and gatekeeping, and some ways in which they come into play within Canadian media, and Canadian news media. Though our media will continue to change overtime, and the ethics and gatekeeping will inevitably change with it, it's important for us to remember that every single piece of media that we take in has been subject to some form of gatekeeping, and it is often up to us to decide, based on our own ethical guidelines, whether or not the gatekeeping that a particular piece of media has been impacted by, was ethical. By carefully considering the information we receive, and the gates it has made it through to end up in our hands, we can better understand the intricate dance that happens between ethics and gatekeeping each and every day.

Conclusion: Gatekeeping and You

As we've explored throughout this book, gatekeeping is a multifaceted and particularly interesting topic to study. From the way it's defined and often compared to other forms of propaganda and censorship to some of the theories behind why it is such a hot-button topic, gatekeeping has proven itself to be a worthy and important topic of conversation. Let's take a quick moment to review some of our learnings, before posing a question to ourselves: how do we recognize and stand up to gatekeeping in our own lives?

The introduction to this book provided us with three important facets of study: communication, rhetoric, and communication theory. As we learned, communication is an oft-overlooked phrase because people think they know exactly what it constitutes and how it works. Taking the time to review definitions of communication and even the Shannon and Weaver model of communication allowed us to ensure all our preconceived notions about communication were set straight before we began our journey through this book. Then, we learned about rhetoric, and some of the ways in which arguments and discussions are organized in order to promote success. Being able to recognize and understand the basic principles of rhetoric becomes particularly important as we explore gatekeeping techniques, as it allows us to understand and refute gatekeeping attempts, if necessary. Finally, we answered what was likely a burning question: why *Canadian* communication theory? By exploring the unique nature of Canadian communication theory, we set ourselves up for success as we moved on to exploring Canadian communication theorists and theories, by understanding some of the basics of how and why their theories are unique to Canada.

In the first chapter, we took some time to consider the differences - in definition and in practice - between gatekeeping, censorship, and propaganda. Much like communication, people often feel they understand the concepts of gatekeeping, censorship, and propaganda, so by breaking those concepts down in our minds and building them back up again, we offered ourselves the chance to ensure that as we continued through this book, that we knew what the major definitional and functional differences were between the three terms. To ensure we knew the difference, we learned about a librarian from the New York Public Library, and explored her vendetta against *Goodnight Moon*, which provided us with a practical way to demonstrate just how impactful gatekeeping, censorship, and propaganda can be within a functional system. Ensuring there were no questions about the three terms was extremely important as we moved on to discussing those concepts within the context of print and digital media.

The second chapter led us through a series of communication theorists and their theories in relation to gatekeeping within print media. We learned about Harold Adams Innis and his staple theory, taking our considerations about gatekeeping all the way back to the sources upon which print materials are created from, which reminded us that gatekeeping is more than just a barrier of a single person. Through discussing Marshall McLuhan's theories about communication and gatekeeping, we learned about how politics and political viewpoints often factor into communication, and began to discuss the concept of truth through McLuhan's discussion on the artist. When we talked about John Grierson, we learned about his concept of democratic propaganda, and his idea that different types of media can be put to use in ways that provide important information to everyday citizens so they can stay accurately informed on hot-button topics. Finally, we were introduced to the communication theory of Gertrude Joch Robinson, and her theories of truth, reality, and gatekeeping through the question: how do we know if something is true? Throughout these explorations, we considered practical examples that enabled us to open our minds to new ways of thinking about gatekeeping in print media.

The third chapter allowed us to switch gears from print to digital media. After establishing the differences between print and digital media, the digital media chapter encouraged us to consider three different types of digital media: documentary film, film and television, and radio. Our discussion on documentary film returned us to discussion surrounding John Grierson and democratic propaganda, since Grierson's preferred method of communication was the documentary film. When we discussed film and television, we learned about the Canadian Broadcasting Corporation, its history, and the ways in which it acts as a gatekeeper vis-à-vis the types of content that are produced and aired in Canada. From there, we discussed radio content, and gatekeeping beyond Canadian borders: how the United States and Canada battled over Canadian content and culture on Canadian radio waves. These discussions centred around the important concept of gatekeeping, and encouraged us to think about the digital content that we take in, and how we consider the amount of gates it has passed through just to be on our radio or TV.

Our fourth and final chapter centred around the ethics of gatekeeping, which is a large, heavy, and controversial topic. After providing context through defining terms like ethics, and ensuring that a fundamental understanding of the connection between ethics and gatekeeping was established, we explored the roles of some common gatekeepers within our communities, like journalists, and what regulations govern their choices. By exploring and understanding these roles, we had a better understanding of the ethical choices that gatekeepers have to make themselves, and some of the choices that are made for them by governing bodies - gatekeepers on another level. Of course, ethics and gatekeeping as a topic alone could fill many books, so taking this brief dive into the topic provided us only with a scratch on the surface on the topic, but with enough of an understanding to complement what had already been provided in regards to communication, gatekeeping, and Canadian media.

Now, after all of this exploration, there is no doubt in any mind that gatekeeping is around us each and every day. The one question that this book has not yet directly addressed is this: what can we do about it? How can we take the time to question and understand each piece of information we receive on a daily basis? To explore this topic, and bring our conversation on gatekeeping, Canadian media, and communication theory to a close, let's talk about one of the most accessible forms of gatekeeping known to the world at this time: social media.

When Marshall McLuhan talked about a global village, social media may not have been what he had in mind, but the phrase global village perfectly encapsulates what social media has become. People share, and often overshare, many if not all aspects of their lives for their friends and the rest of the world to see. In many cases, social media functions as a way to stroke the ego - posting pictures and status updates to demonstrate your success: new job, new publication, new car, pregnancy announcement, and more. In others, it removes the face-to-face aspect of anger, offering the opportunity for so-called keyboard warriors to take to the stage and share their unmasked feelings through what can be a somewhat anonymous channel.

Many things happen on social media that can be considered gatekeeping. Journalists share news stories and live tweet events. Individuals share news articles that support their point of view and debunk those who oppose them. People call out celebrities and other popular figures, often in relation to 'cancel culture,' or an attempt to turn the public against a certain celebrity or figure. People that are angry will send a series of threatening and angry messages, posts, or tweets towards the person or company they are upset with. On the flip side, people share cute pictures of their kids and dogs, talk about important positive things in their lives, and more. The question remains: how can we establish when and where gatekeeping happens within social media?

Our answer is always going to be the same: do your research. Use the tools of rhetoric that we taught you in the introduction to look deeper than just the surface of a message - consider who the person sharing the information is, how reliable a source they are, and what they might have to gain from framing the issue in that particular manner. At the same time, as you see what is on the page, wonder what isn't on the page: consider what might not have been included in the message, and how you might be able to find that information. Obviously you can't do this for each and every message you see each day, but when it comes to important topics, these are just a few tips you can use to ensure that you're getting the full picture.

In addition, use your powers of social media for good. If you see injustice, in terms of gatekeeping or otherwise, use your voice to call for change. If a book by your favourite author has been pulled from the shelves, ask why. If a change was made to a curriculum for your children that softens certain teachings about history, call it out and demand that it be changed. Through social media, your voice can be amplified by others, and you can use that to your advantage to ensure that the people serving you are sharing fair and accurate information across the board.

In closing, the authors of this book encourage you, our dear readers, to continue to learn about gatekeeping in Canadian media. Study the organizations from which you get your information. When you go to a bookstore and see what books are on the shelves, consider what isn't on the shelves, and why they aren't there. You as an individual have the power to create impactful change in your world, and it starts by opening your eyes and questioning the things around you. Take your time, consider which issues are most important to you, and find ways to ensure that if someone wanted to research that issue in full, that they would have the ability to learn about all sides of the issue in a way that permits them to make up their mind themselves. Gatekeeping lives around us constantly, and it is up to us to establish where it exists, how it impacts us, and what we can do about it. If you have learned anything in this book, we hope that it is to be curious, to question things, and to think about why materials exist in the forms they do, with the information they do, in the places that they do.

Works Cited:

1952: CBC Television Debuts. (n.d.). CBC Archives. Retrieved from the CBC website on September 7, 2021: https://www.cbc.ca/archives/entry/1952-cbc-television-debuts

Anastaplo, G. (2020). Censorship [definition]. Retrieved from the Encyclopaedia Britannica website on October 3, 2021: https://www.britannica.com/topic/censorship

Babe, R. (2014). Canadian Communication Thought. Toronto, ON: University of Toronto Press.

Burns, J.E. (1997) Gatekeeping pressures in music radio: The environment of choice. [Conference presentation]. Central States Communication Association annual convention, St. Louis, MO, United States. Retrieved from: https://www2.southeastern.edu/Academics/Faculty/jeburns/gatekeep.html

Cambridge Dictionary (2021). Censorship [definition]. Retrieved from the Cambridge dictionary website on September 17, 2021: https://dictionary.cambridge.org/dictionary/english/censorship

Cambridge Dictionary. (n.d.). Documentary [definition]. Retrieved from the Cambridge Dictionary website on October 2, 2021: https://dictionary.cambridge.org/dictionary/english/documentary

Cambridge Dictionary. (n.d.). Ethic [definition]. Retrieved from the Cambridge Dictionary website on October 2, 2021: https://dictionary.cambridge.org/dictionary/english/ethic

Cambridge Dictionary. (2021). Gatekeeping [definition]. Retrieved from the Cambridge Dictionary website on September 8, 2021: https://dictionary. cambridge.org/dictionary/english/gatekeeping

Cambridge Dictionary. (2021). Propaganda [definition]. Retrieved from the Cambridge Dictionary website on October 3, 2021: https://dictionary. cambridge.org/dictionary/english/propaganda

Canadian Media Producers Association. (2018). Profile 2018: Economic Report on the Screen-Based Media Production Industry in Canada. Retrieved from the CMPA website on October 2, 2021: https://cmpa.ca/ wp-content/uploads/2019/03/Profile-2018.pdf

Canadian Radio-television and Telecommunications Commission. (2002). Canadian content requirements for music on Canadian radio. Retrieved from the CRTC website on September 2, 2021: https://crtc.gc.ca/eng/ cancon/r_cdn.htm

CBC/Radio-Canada. (2019). Looking Ahead - Our new strategic plan 2019-2022. [Annual Report]. Retrieved from the CBC/Radio-Canada website on September 13, 2021: https://cbc.radio-canada.ca/en/impact-and-accountability/finances/annual-reports/ar-2018-2019/accountability-plan/looking-ahead

Cipriani, C. (2014, October 17). The Ethics of Documentary Filmmaking. IndieWire. Retrieved from the IndieWire website on September 4th, 2021: https://www.indiewire.com/2014/10/the-ethics-of-documentary-filmmaking-69007/

Corbett, E. & Connors, R. (1999). Classical Rhetoric for the Modern Student (4th edition). New York, NY: Oxford University Press, Inc.

Davie, G. (n.d.).Gatekeeping Theory [Web log post]. Retrieved from the Mass Comm Theory website on October 2, 2021: https:// masscommtheory.com/theory-overviews/gatekeeping-theory/

Dictionary.com (2021). Gatekeeping [definition]. Retrieved from the Dictionary.com website on September 16, 2021: https://www.dictionary. com/browse/gatekeeper

Encyclopedia.com. (2021). Staples and Staple Theory [article]. Retrieved from the Encyclopedia.com website on September 24, 2021: https://www.encyclopedia.com/history/news-wires-white-papers-and-books/staples-and-staple-theory

Encyclopaedia Britannica (2017). Auteur theory [article]. Retrieved from the Encyclopaedia Britannica website on October 2, 2021: https://www.britannica.com/art/auteur-theory

Gale. (2009). Representations of the Holocaust in Children's Literature. [Encyclopedia Entry]. Retrieved from the Encyclopedia.com website on October 2, 2021: https://www.encyclopedia.com/children/academic-and-educational-journals/representations-holocaust-childrens-literature#Introduction

Goodreads (2021). Historical Fiction [webpage]. Retrieved from the Goodreads website on September 19, 2021: https://www.goodreads.com/genres/historical-fiction

Government of Canada. (2021). The NFB's Mandate Over The Years [webpage]. Retrieved from the Government of Canada website on September 28, 2021: https://www.canada.ca/en/national-film-board/corporate/about/history/mandate-timeline.html

Griffin, E., Ledbetter, A., & Sparks, G. (2015). A First Look at Communication Theory (9th edition). New York, NY: McGraw-Hill Education.

Johannessen L. (2018). Narratives and gatekeeping: making sense of triage nurses' practice. *Sociology of health & illness*, 40(5), 892–906. https://doi.org/10.1111/1467-9566.12732

Kois, D. (2020). How One Librarian Tried to Squash Goodnight Moon [article]. Retrieved from the Slate website on September 16, 2021: https://slate.com/culture/2020/01/goodnight-moon-nypl-10-most-checked-out-books.html

Lees, S. (2016). 5-Point Classical Disposition [PowerPoint Presentation]. Class notes from MacEwan University Communication Studies Class.

Library and Archives Canada (2018). Harold Adams Innis [biography]. Retrieved from the Library and Archives Canada website on September 15, 2021: https://www.bac-lac.gc.ca/eng/discover/military-heritage/first-world-war/100-stories/Pages/innis.aspx

McGowan, M. G. (2012). The People's University of the Air: St. Francis Xavier University Extension, Social Christianity, and the Creation of CJFX. *Acadiensis*, 41(1). Retrieved from https://journals.lib.unb.ca/index.php/Acadiensis/article/view/19072

McIntosh, A., & Cooper, C. (2020). October Crisis [encyclopedia entry]. Retrieved from the Canadian Encyclopedia on September 30, 2021: https://www.thecanadianencyclopedia.ca/en/article/october-crisis

Media Smarts. (n.d.). Ethical Development. [webpage]. Retrieved from the Media Smarts website on September 16, 2021: https://mediasmarts.ca/digital-media-literacy/digital-issues/online-ethics/ethical-development

Merriam-Webster. (2021). Censor [definition] Retrieved from the Merriam-Webster website on October 3, 2021: https://www.merriam-webster.com/dictionary/medium

Merriam-Webster. (2021). Medium [definition] Retrieved from the Merriam-Webster website on September 20, 2021: https://www.merriam-webster.com/dictionary/medium

Merriam-Webster. (2021). Propaganda [definition]. Retrieved from the Merriam-Webster website on October 3, 2021: https://www.merriam-webster.com/dictionary/propaganda

Nelson, L., & Nelson., T. (1999). Learning History Through Children's Literature [article]. Retrieved from the ERIC Digest website on October 2, 2021: https://www.ericdigests.org/2000-3/history.htm

Nichols, B. (2006, April 30). What to Do About Documentary Distortion? Toward a Code of Ethics. International Documentary Association. Retrieved from the IDA website on August 28, 2021: https://www.documentary.org/feature/what-do-about-documentary-distortion-toward-code-ethics

Shade, L. (n.d.). The Tradition of Canadian Communication Theory [article]. Retrieved from the Info America website on September 13, 2021: https://www.infoamerica.org/documentos_pdf/smythe02.pdf

Singer, J.B. (2008). The Journalist in the Network. A Shifting Rationale for the Gatekeeping Role and the Objectivity Norm. Tripodos, 23, 61-76.

Smith, B. (2021). Propaganda [article]. Retrieved from the Encyclopaedia Britannica website on September 18, 2021: https://www.britannica.com/topic/propaganda

Stiehm, J. (2014). A Life in Full [article]. Retrieved from the Swarthmore College website on September 18, 2021: https://www.swarthmore.edu/bulletin/archive/wp/april-2014_a-life-in-full.html

Through the Years. (n.d.). CBC Radio Website. Retrieved from the CBC Radio website on September 14, 2021: https://cbc.radio-canada.ca/en/your-public-broadcaster/history

United States Holocaust Memorial Museum (2021). Nazi Propaganda [article]. Retrieved from the United States Holocaust Memorial Museum website on September 18, 2021: https://encyclopedia.ushmm.org/content/en/article/nazi-propaganda

University of Arkansas (n.d.). The Five Canons of Rhetoric [webpage]. Retrieved from the University of Arkansas website on August 16, 2021: https://walton.uark.edu/business-communication-lab/Resources/downloads/The_Five_Canons_of_Rhetoric.pdf

Urban Dictionary. (2012). Gatekeeping [definition]. Retrieved from the Urban Dictionary website on September 8, 2021:https://www.urbandictionary.com/define.php?term=Gatekeeping

Vargas, B. (2019). Art and Discipline [blog post]. Retrieved from the SUNY Geneseo website on August 16, 2021: https://morrison.sunygeneseoenglish.org/2019/02/17/art-and-discipline/

Wandering, G. (2015). Gatekeepers: Who Holds the Power to Get Your Film Made [webpage]. Retrieved from the Waondering website on October 2, 2021: https://waondering.com/2015/11/29/gate-keeper-who-holds-the-power-to-get-your-film-made/